PLANT RELOCATION

A Case History of a Move

ABOUT THE AUTHORS

Edmund S. Whitman is retired vice president for public relations of the United Fruit Company. He started as a timekeeper on a banana plantation and during 40 years of service with the company worked in both tropical and domestic departments in agriculture, marketing, sales, advertising, and public relations.

Mr. Whitman received his education at M.I.T. and Williams College. He is the author of three novels; a travel book; and numerous short stories, magazine articles, and newspaper columns. He has also written and directed several motion pictures.

W. James Schmidt, a senior public relations specialist for General Foods Corporation, White Plains, New York, was formerly manager of community relations at the company's Jell-O Division plant in Dover, Delaware.

A graduate of the School of Journalism, University of Florida, Schmidt was a reporter and editor for the Gainesville, Florida, *Daily Sun,* the Wilmington, Delaware, *Journal,* and the Army Times Publishing Co.

From 1957 to 1961 he was chief of information for the Highway Research Board, National Academy of Sciences, at a road research project in Illinois. Prior to joining General Foods in 1963, he was an information officer for the Bureau of Public Roads, U.S. Department of Commerce.

PLANT RELOCATION

A Case History of a Move

By

Edmund S. Whitman

W. James Schmidt

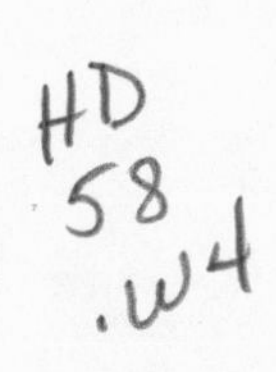

AMERICAN MANAGEMENT ASSOCIATION

NEW YORK

This book has been distributed without charge to AMA members
enrolled in the General Management Division. Those members
who are enrolled in other divisions, or who wish extra copies,
may order the book in a hardcover edition at $5 per copy.
Price to nonmembers, $7.50.

Library of Congress catalog card number: 66-16532

Map design by Henri Fluchere.

FOREWORD

In March 1962 General Foods Corporation announced that its board of directors had authorized funds for site selection and preliminary engineering for a new food processing plant to be located within 250 miles of New York City. The new facility—part of the company's Jell-O Division—would replace four older plants located in the northeastern part of the United States and would consolidate all of their various operations under one roof.

Six months later the company announced the selection of Dover, Delaware, as the site for the new plant. Construction began in October 1962, and the first products came off the lines in January 1964. As production at the new plant increased, operations at the old plants were gradually phased out. More than 2,000 major pieces of equipment were moved to the new plant; approximately 500 employees transferred to the new location or to other General Foods plants, while some 1,300 terminated, retired, or resigned. The new plant, formally dedicated in May 1965, represented the largest capital investment in the company's history.

From the beginning, General Foods was determined to make this massive move of machines and people as near perfect an operation as possible—to make it, in a sense, a textbook case study in plant relocation. This, in turn, suggested the desirability of making available to other managers, who might also be faced with the difficult and complex task of plant relocation, a permanent record of the reasons for the move, the planning involved, how the actual move was made, a summary of lessons that were learned, and general guidelines that might prove useful in similar circumstances.

General Foods was eager to cooperate in such an endeavor because of the frustration it had experienced in searching library shelves in vain for definitive case history material on plant moves and consolidations. There was little or nothing to help solve the many financial, manufacturing, engineering, marketing, personnel, and public relations problems that arose in connection with the move.

The American Management Association had for some time sensed the need for a book that would provide its members and other interested managers with the benefits of a practical experience in plant relocation. Moreover, the project agreed fully with its basic policy of serving as a channel of communication between managers.

The authors wish to acknowledge the help and encouragement they have received from both General Foods and the American Management Association in the writing and publication of this book. General Foods permitted free access to people, facts, and figures—with the sole limitation being applied to disclosure of specific figures on capital expenditures, operating costs, and savings related to the move to the new plant. The American Management Association provided the services and advice of its editorial staff in the complicated process of bringing forth a new book. It is the hope of all concerned that managers will find in this volume help and guidance in solving their own problems of plant relocation.

CONTENTS

AN IDEA TAKES SHAPE

Chapter I

AN IDEA TAKES SHAPE

General Foods Corporation, one of the nation's largest producers of packaged convenience foods, was formed by a series of consolidations and acquisitions dating back to 1925 when the Postum Cereal Company of Battle Creek, Michigan, was consolidated with the Jell-O Company of LeRoy, New York. In subsequent years, a number of independent companies—all producing familiar, brand-name products—joined the organization: Igleheart Brothers (Swans Down) and Minute Tapioca in 1926; Franklin Baker Coconut, Walter Baker Chocolate, and Log Cabin Syrup in 1927; Maxwell House Coffee, La France (laundry products), and Calumet Baking Powder in 1928. The organization took the name "General Foods" in 1929. Since then, other well-known companies have joined the corporation: Birds Eye, Gaines Dog Foods, Kool-Aid, Good Seasons, and S.O.S., for example.

Over the years the company has experienced a steady growth. In the fiscal year which ended March 31, 1965, net sales were approximately $1.5 billion, marking an increase in net sales and net earnings for the thirteenth consecutive year. It was also the forty-third year in which the company had paid a dividend to stockholders each quarter. The company had approximately 30,000 employees and 77,000 stockholders; operated more than 60 plants, warehouses, and offices in the United States; and had subsidiary operations in 17 foreign countries.

General Foods has a decentralized operating structure organized in eight domestic divisions and subsidiary companies overseas. The divisions are Jell-O, Maxwell House, Post, Birds Eye, Kool-Aid, Institutional Food Service, International, and Distribution-Sales Services. Although each division has headquarters at the company's main offices in White Plains, New York, it functions independently in production, operations, and marketing. All common functions such as advertising are correlated at the corporate level by appropriate staff departments. Warehousing and shipping are handled through a nationwide network of 25 sales-distribution facilities. More than 200 products are marketed under 30 major brand names.

The Jell-O Division, which takes its name from the famous gelatin dessert, also produces puddings, dessert toppings, and coconut, rice, tapioca, syrup, and chocolate products. In 1960 the division had five principal plants processing and packaging its various grocery and industrial products as well as certain institutional items. These plants were Franklin Baker in Hoboken, New Jersey; Walter Baker in Dorchester, Massachusetts; the Minute Rice and Tapioca Plant at Orange, Massachusetts; Jell-O at LeRoy, New York; and Calumet in Chicago, Illinois. The division also operated Atlantic Gelatin in Woburn, Massachusetts, and Hollywood, California; Northland Dairy in Evart, Michigan; and a coconut-processing plant in San Pablo, Philippines. In addition, some Jell-O Division products were processed and packaged in Maxwell House Division plants in Houston, Texas, and San Leandro, California.

All five of the division's main plants had been acquired in the late 1920's. Some buildings, although extensively revamped and altered, had been constructed before the acquisitions and were part of the original, family-owned businesses.

Perhaps the most famous of the division's plants was the Walter Baker Chocolate Company, which was founded in 1765 in Dorchester, Massachusetts—a suburb of Boston in later years. It had the distinction of being the oldest concern in the United States with a record of having made the same type of product continuously in its original location. Some of the Walter Baker buildings dated back to the mid-nineteenth century.

The Franklin Baker Coconut Company got its start in 1895 in Philadelphia. Franklin Baker (no relation to Walter Baker) was a flour merchant who received a shipment of fresh coconuts from Cuba in payment of a debt. Unable to find a buyer, he purchased a small coconut-processing business. The enterprise flourished, moved to Brooklyn, and, in 1924, to Hoboken, New Jersey.

The Minute Tapioca Company originated in 1894 in the kitchen of a Boston boardinghouse keeper who used her coffee grinder to remove lumps from tapioca. Her smooth-textured puddings became so famous that they caught the attention of John Whitman, owner of a newspaper in Orange, Massachusetts, who bought the rights to use the process. He established the Whitman Grocery Company in Orange and called his product Tapioca Superlative. The name was changed to Minute Tapioca a year or so later, and in 1902 Whitman and others purchased a former shoe factory and converted it into a tapioca plant. The company joined the future General Foods organization in 1926.

Jell-O can be traced back to 1845 to a patent obtained by Peter Cooper, inventor of the famous "Tom Thumb" locomotive. However, it really came into being in LeRoy, New York, in 1897 in the kitchen of Pearl B. Wait, a manufacturer of cough medicine, and his wife, May. Two years later Wait sold out, for a mere $450, to a man named Orator Woodward. By 1902 Woodward had Jell-O sales up to a quarter of a million dollars, and the rest is history. When the Postum Cereal Company was consolidated with Jell-O in 1925, the Jell-O business was valued at about $70 million.

Calumet Baking Powder was born in Chicago in 1889 under the guidance of a young food salesman named William M. Wright, who began making the product in a combination laboratory, office, and bedroom. Wright's business grew rapidly, outgrowing its first plant by 1902 and needing still more factory space in 1912. The company became a part of General Foods in 1928.

These five plants—Dorchester, Orange, LeRoy, Hoboken, and Chicago—became the backbone of Jell-O Division manufacturing facilities. All had been acquired in the 1920's; all were, at least in part, old and outmoded; none was at a location chosen by General Foods. Some had grown over the years by the process of "tacking on" additions as needed; some had undergone extensive structural changes to accommodate new equipment. The Walter Baker plant was a sprawling complex of some 20 buildings separated from each other by a city street and a river. Franklin Baker and Calumet were multistoried, "vertical" plants, inefficient when compared to modern, horizontal plant layouts. All three of these plants were in crowded urban areas where expansion would mean acquiring high-cost land. The Jell-O and Minute plants, even though located in small towns, were hemmed in by railroad tracks, streets, and —at LeRoy—a cemetery.

The division, then, was faced with the problem of a growing, dynamic business which over the years had been crowded bit by bit into the existing plants. It had become obvious that production facilities needed to be extensively revamped and revitalized if the division's competative position was to be maintained and provisions made for new processes and products. There were many discussions and informal studies of the problem, and it is difficult to pinpoint the origin of the idea of closing one or more of the old plants and building a new consolidated facility. Many months of painstaking study were required before the final course became clear and the move toward consolidation became a reality.

Studies began in early 1960, when steps were taken to set up a task force to make an exploratory investigation and to establish a steering committee to guide and review progress of the work. The task force was composed of one man from each of the division's major operating areas, one from the division controller's department, and one from the corporate manufacturing and engineering area. The steering committee was composed of the operations managers of four plants—Walter Baker, Franklin Baker, Jell-O, and Minute.

In outlining the basis for a broad study of all production facilities, one member of the steering committee listed the following "desires of the division" and recommended their consideration:

1. The Jell-O Division, while it recognizes the need for foresight in facilities planning, must maintain an acceptable profit and thus desires to establish new and/or enlarged facilities within the limits of its ability to produce such profits.
2. Except where other overriding advantages prevail, the Jell-O Division prefers to expand facilities at present manufacturing locations rather than to establish new locations with duplication of overhead costs.
3. Other things being equal, the Jell-O Division prefers to manufacture its own products [rather than use "co-pack" operations].
4. The Jell-O Division does not desire to discontinue present operations unless the study indicates substantial economic and other advantages in doing so.
5. The Jell-O Division requires facilities that are sufficiently flex-

ible to accommodate processes for [as yet] unidentifiable new products.
6. Facilities should be planned to provide for installation of modern processes for producing Jell-O products.

The task force began its study with instructions "to develop possible alternatives for the future production of Jell-O Division products based on the economic purchase of raw materials, the optimum distribution of finished goods, the use of improved physical facilities—including modernized equipment and relocated and consolidated plants—and the comparison of the advantages of these alternatives with the advantages of remaining at the existing locations."

Thus the task force started its study with no predisposition toward a massive shutdown and consolidation. Improvement of existing facilities was still very much in the picture, and the idea of abandoning one or more of the old plants was approached with caution. However, consolidation quickly leaped to the forefront of task force thinking as it became clear that the investment of more and more money in the outmoded plants would be unsound. As Charles G. Mortimer, then chairman, put it:

> The economics clearly dictated consolidation. It had become demonstrably unprofitable to try to keep step with today's fierce competition in acquired structures and locations that had outlived their practicality. The opportunities inherent in massive consolidation at a site of the company's own choosing were simply not to be denied.

The small task force obviously could not provide quick and easy answers to the multitude of questions raised by a proposed consolidation—questions in the field of engineering, sales, marketing, employee relations, public relations, and so forth. Thus it chose to stick closely to the overriding consideration—that is, what course of action would be most likely to lead to maximum cost reductions and the greatest increase in profits?

The task force study was conducted in six phases:

1. Analysis of transportation costs and product allocation.
2. Estimate of construction costs for new facilities.
3. Estimate of overhead staffing of new facilities.
4. Comparison of direct costs at new facilities with existing costs.
5. Estimate of shutdown, employee-termination, and start-up costs.
6. Development of profit and loss projections.

In October 1960 the division operations manager, Robert A. Stringer, who headed the steering committee, reported to the general manager, E. Burke Giblin, that the first step in the study had been completed. This "rough estimate" of transportation and raw materials costs indicated that "substantial savings are possible." From this encouraging beginning, the task force proceeded to studies dealing with overhead costs, direct labor costs, maintenance, capital expenditures, and so on.

The task force made its first formal report to the steering committee in February 1961, summarizing the results as follows:

> The first step was to determine the optimum general geographic location in the United States for facilities to replace the five major Jell-O Division plants. Eliminating the Far West (to be the subject of a separate study), three geographical areas were considered —the South, East, and Midwest.
>
> The initial effort proved that a seperate Southern plant location was not economically advantageous at the present time because it merely replaced one existing facility, and direct and transportation savings were not sufficient to justify the investment.
>
> It became apparent that the most significant savings were obtainable through overhead reductions by consolidation of existing Jell-O plants into fewer plants. The overhead savings that have been identified represent approximately 80 percent of the total savings of this study. Direct and transportation savings represent the remainder.

In other words, the task force saw that consolidation was clearly the key to major cost reductions and increased profits. Each of the old plants had its own personnel department, quality control staff, production planning and scheduling, accountants, maintenance forces, storekeepers, warehousemen, guards and watchmen, janitors, and so on. Consolidation would centralize many of these functions, thus reducing the number of people needed and cutting costs correspondingly.

The task force considered four consolidation plans:

1. A two-plant combination with one new plant in the East, including the major manufacturing facilities of the chocolate operation, and one new plant in the Midwest.
2. The same as combination No. 1 but with the expansion of Calumet (Chicago) instead of a completely new Midwestern facility.
3. A three-plant combination consisting of one new plant in the East, the major chocolate-manufacturing facility remaining at Dorchester, and one new plant in the Midwest.

4. The same as No. 3 but with the expansion of Calumet instead of the completely new Midwestern facility.

The task force estimated significant savings—several million dollars per year—for any of the four alternatives and payback times running from 10.9 to 12.2 years.

On the basis of these encouraging findings, the task force recommended continuing the study along the following lines:

- Other alternatives were to be developed to assure that savings would be optimal and the adverse effect on profit minimized.
- The proposed overhead organization was to be explored in detail to determine whether all functions were adequately staffed.
- Since the manufacturing and engineering estimate of new plant cost was preliminary only, further engineering studies were to be authorized if the study were continued.
- The assumptions made for justification of new equipment were to be verified and any additional equipment and process improvements identified.
- Other factors relating to the abandonment of existing facilities were to be explored.
- Criteria were to be developed for selecting specific geographic locations and sites for any proposed facility.
- A specific timetable with a corresponding plan of action embracing all phases of any future study was to be developed.

The division's general manager passed along the preliminary results to top management. "I believe," he wrote, "the only conclusion we can draw at this time is that the figures appear interesting enough to warrant further study and review. This is under way." Management agreed, and money was provided to continue the study as recommended.

One month later two additional consolidation alternatives were proposed by the task force: (1) a total of three plants—one new Eastern; Calumet as is; Dorchester as is or (2) a total of two plants—one new Eastern with the chocolate facility and Calumet as is.

Again the consolidation plans produced favorable estimates of annual savings, return, and payback, and the task force was now able to proceed with comparisons among the alternatives. Its conclusions were that a new Midwest facility was not justified; an expanded Midwest facility was not justified; and the move of the chocolate operation to a consolidated Eastern plant *was* justified.

In other words, the task force studies pointed to the sixth alternative —one new Eastern plant combining all four old Eastern plants, with

Calumet as it was—as the only justifiable plan. Estimated annual savings for this plan were near the top of the range for all alternatives; payback time was estimated at less than ten years; and the estimated effect on division profits at the end of 15 years was the best of all alternatives.

The task force study was now essentially completed and, in terms of savings and potential profit increases, the plan to combine the four Eastern plants looked good. It was also obvious that such a consolidation offered advantages in providing for future expansion, for achieving greater flexibility to meet unforeseen conditions and consumer demands, and in general for maintaining the competitive leadership of the company.

However, the plan had some negative aspects, too. General Foods had been in the four old communities for many years, and the plants with their brand-name products had been community fixtures for even more years. It was obviously not going to be easy to pull up these deep, historic roots and move away to some as-yet-unidentified spot. Shutting the doors of the old plants was bound to have a detrimental effect on community economy, particularly in the small towns of Orange and LeRoy. Many experienced employees would no doubt be unable to move with their jobs, and long-nurtured community relations would inevitably be jeopardized.

Another disadvantage was the danger of putting all of Jell-O's manufacturing eggs in one basket. The proposed consolidated plant would handle approximately two-thirds of the entire production of the division; and Jell-O division products were found in more homes in the United States than any other brands of grocery items. A work stoppage, whether caused by labor union action or by some natural disaster, would obviously be much more serious than such an occurrence at one of the old plants.

In this connection, there was the question of union organization of a consolidated plant. Two of the existing plants, Hoboken and Dorchester, were union-organized; LeRoy and Orange were not, and attempts to organize them had failed. Since Hoboken and Dorchester were by far the larger of the four plants, they would undoubtedly produce the bulk of transferring employees. Therefore, it seemed quite likely that union organization would be attempted early at a consolidated plant. Labor-management relationships in the old plants had, however, been harmonious for many years, and unionization of the proposed new plant seemed to pose no great problems for the company.

The task force's final assessment of the overall situation was:

> The alternative that best protects the future of the business—and the future of all of us who work for it—is now obvious.
>
> Figures on alternate consolidations show several that would improve our current position. For instance, consideration was given to the possibility of keeping the two union-operated plants of Dorchester and Hoboken where they are and consolidating the other two. But an examination of the long-term results reveals the shortcomings of any such course of action. We'd just be postponing the problem, ending up with two outmoded plants instead of four.
>
> The end result of Phase I is, therefore, to recommend going all out for the consolidation of the four plants under one roof and to do it with the realization that management has full understanding of the risks inherent in such an "eggs in one basket" undertaking. (Management decided that the advantages of consolidation far outweighed the risk.)

Of course, many questions remained unanswered at this point in the study. For example, how sound and accurate were the estimates of capital expenditure, savings, payback, and profit made by the task force? How much existing equipment *could* be moved from the old plants? How much *should* be moved? What would be the magnitude of inventory buildup needed to assure a normal flow of products to grocery store shelves during the shutdown and start-up period?

There were questions concerning the new plant. In general, what should be its size and layout? Should there be space for potential new products and how much? Should the industrial sales department be located at the new plant or at corporate headquarters? What about the research department? What technological improvements were to be incorporated into the new plant? Where should it be built? Should consultants be employed to assist in site selection. Should it be built in conjunction with one of the company's distribution-sales warehouses?

There were also personnel and public relations questions. What transfer, termination, and retirement policies should be followed with regard to employees in the old plants? What impact would the plant shutdowns have in the four communities? What could be done to soften the blow? What advance preparations should public relations make in the old as well as the new plant communities?

These questions, and many others, needed definitive answers before any firm consolidation proposal could be made to corporate management and, ultimately, to the board of directors. However, top management had been kept informed of the progress and posted on the final results of the task force study. Management approved, and the go-ahead signal was given.

This early and continuing managerial approval was a great incentive to the men who had been spending full time on the facilities study. Further stimulation came when the Jell-O Division management made it clear that those who made significant contributions and recommendations would have the opportunity to implement their ideas in the new plant. In other words, the key people in planning would be the key people in making the plans work, and there was every likelihood of this leading to increased responsibility and promotion.

Communication with top management was highly important. In later stages of the study, the Jell-O Division maintained close contact with General Foods President, C. W. Cook who, in turn, was part of the company's operating policy committee which included Charles G. Mortimer, chairman; Herbert M. Cleaves, executive vice president—marketing; and Arthur E. Larkin, Jr., executive vice president—operations. Mr. Cook, who ultimately succeeded Mr. Mortimer as chief executive, provided the principal liaison with the company's board of directors.

One of the final moves of the task force was to furnish management with information to help in assessing the economic effects of the shutdowns in the four old communities. Obviously, the closing of the plants in Hoboken and Dorchester, while critical for the approximately 1,300 employees involved, would cause scarcely a ripple in the overall economy of these two urban industrial areas. Orange with a population of only 6,000 and LeRoy with a population of 6,800 were different cases. The effects were bound to be much greater, and this was a point of considerable concern in top management ranks.

LeRoy had five industries, including the Jell-O plant, employing approximately 1,500 people. Thus Jell-O's 370 employees represented about 25 percent of the total industrial employment in the town. It appeared that a shutdown at Jell-O would be a serious blow to the economy. However, the figures were tempered somewhat by LeRoy's proximity to Batavia and Rochester, where there were large industries which might absorb some of the excess labor. In addition, there were indications that another LeRoy industry was about to expand, which would put it in the market for additional employees.

Orange had 12 small plants employing about 925 people. The Minute plant with 97 employees accounted for about 10 percent of the total.

But, again, a look at a broader area showed a different picture. Orange is three miles from Athol, and the two towns are so interrelated that they could be considered one community. The total industrial employment in Orange-Athol was 4,250. Thus the Minute plant accounted for only about two percent of the work force in the larger community.

Of course, figures alone did not tell the whole story, as is evidenced by the following memo from the operations manager at the Jell-O plant:

> The Jell-O plant in LeRoy has been in existence since 1897. It is the oldest active industry in the area. Jell-O *is* General Foods, as far as the local community is concerned. Jell-O is considered the leading industry and the most desirable place to work. It is the one industry in the local area offering a relatively large number of desirable factory jobs to women.
>
> The Jell-O plant has been, and still is, a vital part of the total community. It is the parent plant of Jell-O. Its original owners built their fortunes in the Jell-O business and left their impact on the economic, social, educational, and spiritual life of the community through personal leadership and liberal philanthropies. General Foods continues to lead in its support of community activities.
>
> Jell-O employees have a record of long service with 36 having 25 years or more of continuous employment. Basically, Jell-O employees live in the village and town, with more than 95 percent living within a ten-mile radius of the plant.

Nonetheless, the General Foods management faced up to the decision to move ahead with the study and to abandon the old plants if necessary. The decision to leave the four older communities was a difficult one, but one which any management faced with the same set of circumstances would be forced to make. Otherwise, it would have been remiss in its obligations to the company, its stockholders, and its employees.

The task force and its steering committee officially completed their assignment on July 1, 1961. What had been an idea was now approaching a plan; but it was a plan that needed many months of intensive study before further action could be taken. Accordingly, the task force recommended setting up an organizational unit within the Jell-O Division to continue the work. The task force had broken the ground and laid out the guidelines; now the real digging was to begin.

THE IDEA BECOMES A PLAN

Chapter II

THE IDEA BECOMES A PLAN

The first assessment of consolidation possibilities was now in hand, and Jell-O Division management decided to proceed with further and more detailed studies. Acting on the task force recommendations, Jell-O set up a facilities improvement group, and the manufacturing and engineering manager of one of GF's Midwest plants was called in to direct its operation. His first report to management reflected both the prevailing spirit of optimism and a realization of the tremendous problems ahead:

> All efforts to date indicate a favorable payback on the consolidation of the division's four Eastern plants into one new facility; and, if we assume this actually proves to be the case, we are faced with a highly complex effort in terms of the large number of factors and wide variety of problems and interests involved in accomplishing this most effectively. This would present us with the

most challenging opportunity in the division's history for operational improvement. It would be a situation where we would need to draw upon our total divisional and corporate pool of experience to be sure that the facility and staffing be unexcelled.

Accordingly, a six-phase program was outlined for carrying the work forward through construction of the new plant, shutdown of the old plants, and startup of the consolidated facility. Phase I was the already completed task force feasibility study. The remaining phases were as follows:

Phase II—savings and cost verification—doing *only* that work necessary to justify or reject a recommendation for building a new Eastern plant consolidating the Hoboken, Dorchester, LeRoy, and Orange operations and, if indicated, to obtain board approval of required funds for preliminary engineering.

Phase III—preliminary engineering—doing all engineering work necessary to finalize costs and savings, identify and institute new-equipment developments, undertake site selection, and obtain approval for final engineering.

Phase IV—final engineering and appropriation request—doing all engineering work for the complete facility and preparing an appropriation request.

Phase V—construction—building the facility according to developed specifications and within approved time and budget and developing the final scheduling required for facility startup.

Phase VI—shutdown and startup—transferring production from existing lines to the new facility with a minimum of lost efficiency and according to developed schedules so that no out-of-stock situations occur.

Since the possibility of tremendous savings had been only loosely estimated by the task force, the obvious first step for the facilities improvement group was to refine these figures into a solid estimate. Only then would the group proceed to site selection, precise plant layout, establishment of definite shutdown and start-up schedules, identification of new equipment, and so forth. Thus the facilities improvement manager proposed that the following steps be taken in Phase II:

1. Develop preliminary general plant layout on the basis of using *only* proved equipment (new equipment developments would be provided for in Phase III).
2. Develop manning tables and an administrative organization plan to establish overhead savings.

3. Re-estimate construction costs.
4. Determine what improvement could be made at existing locations.
5. Compare cost and savings of new facility with the best that could be done at existing facilities and calculate payback.
6. Develop time schedules.

At this stage of the study the facilities improvement group was a small unit. So all of the work except that in Step 4 was assigned to the corporate engineering department and accomplished in cooperation with contacts named by the operations managers of the plants. The plant operations managers were asked to assist by listing the improvement possibilities at their locations.

By December 1961 it was apparent that the new facility could have a tremendous effect on the Jell-O Division's profits. There would, of course, be an adverse effect during the start-up period but greatly increased profits once the new plant was running smoothly. It seemed important to identify and resolve as many problems as possible as soon as possible. Therefore, the facilities study group prepared a report for management outlining what it had been doing, how the work was being done, the results to date, and the course for the future.

The factors studied in order to develop costs and savings (Phase II) were listed as follows:

1. Timetable. A detailed schedule for the entire project was developed on the assumption that the facility will effect substantial savings and should, therefore, be completed as quickly as possible. The timetable would require interim approvals for starting Phases III and IV.
2. Equipment selection. All present equipment was reviewed with the respective operations areas and corporate engineering, and agreement was reached on what types of new equipment—no development required—could be included without risk of major delays in startup.
3. Process flow. A complete set of flow charts was developed on the basis of using proved equipment and handling techniques.
4. General plant arrangement. Block types of layouts were developed so that industrial engineering could determine the most effective arrangements for materials handling, labor savings, and general layout.
5. Manning charts. Complete charts—direct and indirect—were developed in cooperation with the operations areas.
6. Administrative organization. With the assistance of the division

personnel department, the general structure was selected and specific staffing recommendations were requested from those expert in their respective areas.

7. Line drawings. Drawings were made to show building size and type, equipment location, floor loading and utility requirements, and so forth, so that a reliable building cost estimate could be made.
8. Savings and expense review. A profit and loss projection was based on current data.

The profit and loss projection included a large loss on the sale of the four old plants. This figure was based on an estimate of sale value made by an industrial real estate consultant and a "write down" to appraised value rather than book value.

Nonetheless, the potential savings still looked good, perhaps not quite as good as those projected from the "guesstimates" of the task force, but still good enough to warrant an air of urgency and full speed ahead on further phases of the project. In addition, the study group felt that the new facility would result in a significant reduction in material losses over the operations being conducted at the four old plants.

Much of the detailed work included in the December 1961 report had been assigned by the Jell-O Division to the corporate manufacturing and engineering department. In several major areas, this department —working with other corporate and plant personnel—had contributed substantially to bringing the study to a proper conclusion. The major areas of responsibility for the Jell-O Division were to:

1. Develop with the Jell-O Division and plant personnel the sales volume by product for the peak quarter at the fiscal-1962, -1968, and -1970 levels of production.
2. Establish inventory levels for all raw materials, packing materials, and finished goods at the fiscal-1970 production level.
3. Determine volume movement and manpower requirements on a day in the peak quarter for the handling of bulk and packaged raw materials, packing materials, and finished goods.

Work assigned to corporate engineering included:

1. Determine the gross area of the warehouse, including the number of truck doors and rail spots.
2. Determine the volume movement of packaged raw materials, packing materials, and finished goods handled on the first floor and the elevator requirements to handle materials on the upper floors.

3. Develop the materials handling requirements for all packaged goods.
4. Develop the manpower requirements for all functions reporting to the manager of manufacturing and engineering. This summary was to note requirements for all direct and indirect jobs, salaried and hourly rated, male and female, as a single plant and split to show the effect on a Jell-O plant and on a seperate chocolate plant.
5. Develop an engineering budget covering the expense of plant, process and project engineering, maintenance, plant services, utilities, and stores.
6. Develop the gross area of the engineering shops and a layout of the shop area.
7. Prepare a financial evaluation of the cost savings of cocoa bean silos versus a conventional cocoa bean warehouse.

Some insight into the complexity of the proposed consolidation can be gained from the schedule proposed by corporate manufacturing and engineering, which reported:

> In preparing the schedule, consideration was given to expediting the changeover from the existing to the new location. In order to minimize the interruption of production, it is planned to purchase certain key items of equipment—over and above that expected to be replaced—which will enable operations for certain products to continue at both the old and new locations during the changeover.
>
> In preparing the schedule, the following assumptions were made for the various products:
>
> > Jell-O Gelatins and Puddings—The equipment for these products is all new and operations can continue at the existing location until the new facility is in complete operation.
> >
> > Bulk Sugar, Gelatin, and Cornstarch—All new equipment is provided, and no interruption in production is anticipated.
> >
> > Minute Tapioca—The equipment to be moved will require that this product be produced in two or three shifts at the existing location prior to relocation in order to build up an inventory.
> >
> > Minute Rice—It is assumed that this product can be produced at the Houston, Texas, Plant during the transfer period.
> >
> > Certo—This is a seasonal pack, and it is assumed that this product will continue to be co-packed until the new facility is completed.

> Jell-O Carton Plant—All of the existing equipment is to be relocated . . . if ample production cannot be maintained during the relocation, it is assumed that cartons can be purchased.*
>
> Log Cabin Syrup—The relocation of this equipment will require additional shifts at Hoboken to build up an inventory, and/or Calumet Plant will have to provide the necessary requirements.
>
> Coconut Products—The majority of the equipment will be relocated from the existing facility. In order to maintain production, even at a reduced level, it is planned to move this process in three stages.
>
> Chocolate Products—It is planned to move the required equipment in two stages. One-half will be moved and started up, and then the remaining equipment.

By the end of 1961 all the data needed for financial analysis had been gathered, and the facilities improvement group outlined its plans for further work leading up to a presentation of its findings to the company's operating policy committee in early 1962. This presentation was to include (1) complete information on payback, return on funds, and profit and loss projection for the new facility on the basis of fiscal 1965—not the point of greatest return for the new facility since it would be designed for the expected production of fiscal 1970; (2) identification of the costs and savings involved in improving the existing plants and a listing of the disadvantages of this course—such as the fact that facilities would still be poorly arranged and incapable of guaranteeing the efficiency of a new plant, that consolidation savings would not be possible, and that sanitation and housekeeping would still present a problem; (3) an estimate of costs involved in providing extra manufacturing space in the new facility for future new products; and (4) an estimate of costs involved in providing research facilities in case it was decided to move divisional research to the new plant.

There was a growing air of urgency in regard to the proposed plant. Potential savings appeared so attractive that a "full speed ahead" feeling developed among those involved in the study, and they recommended going ahead with certain critical phases of their work immediately. For example, new equipment development work and process development work had to be under way in order that new information

*This operation was eventually relocated to GF's Carton and Container Operation in Saratoga Springs, New York, rather than being transferred to the new plant.

would be available for the final engineering of Phase IV. Site selection work had to be started immediately, since the schedule was based upon having made a selection and acquired an option by June 1, 1962. Finally, work had to start on plans for communicating to plant personnel and the old communities the news of the impending move. These plans were to include all policies on moving and details as to why, when, where, who, and so forth. All this information had to be made available as quickly as possible after management made its decision, since the facilities improvement group would then need to begin working closely with people in the affected plants.

The facilities improvement group also asked for fast action on several other problems which would be encountered if and when it moved into Phase III (preliminary engineering). It outlined these as follows:

1. We would need to make available full-time help on the plant engineering, industrial engineering, personnel, and financial elements of the work would be required. Corporate engineering could handle the construction work, but the Jell-O Division would want to handle all aspects of the work concerned with putting the new plant into operation and closing the old facilities. For example, it would want to establish jobs, job descriptions, training requirements, methods, controls, and so on.
2. Equipment with long delivery times should be ordered ahead of the final engineering phase to assure that the schedule could be met.
3. Sales volume projections for present products should be developed as accurately as possible, and future marketing plans and philosophy should be considered with respect to possible effects on facility planning.
4. Research testing and approval would be required for several processing changes which would improve operating efficiencies and general estimates as to what operating problems might be visualized for new products.
5. There would be a continual need for assistance on all financial problems. Methods work and automation studies should be started very early in order to engineer and install the necessary facilities and institute the technique for most efficient operations.

On February 13, 1962, the facilities improvement group submitted a report to the Jell-O Division operating manager who, with the general manager, reported to the operating policy committee prior to its presentation to the board of directors. Months of hard work had gone into the report, and it represented the combined thinking of engineers, accountants, marketing men, personnel men, and plant managers. In a preface to the report, the Jell-O Division operations manager described the consolidation idea as follows:

> It is one which we are approaching with a great deal of enthusiasm. Nevertheless, we recognize that it brings with it very difficult and challenging problems since it involves such large numbers of people and so much of our total operations.
>
> It is not something we *have* to do now. It is at this time a pure cost-saving project. We believe, however, that the timing is right both from an operating and tax point of view.
>
> Four years from now the new plant can represent—from a profit-before-taxes point of view—the equivalent of a new product of about four million units.
>
> Because of this importance we have assigned several of our key men full time to the project, and we are using each of our key operations managers. In addition, we are relying heavily on corporate manufacturing and engineering, not only for advice and counsel each step of the way, but for the actual construction of the facility.

The structure of the report is outlined below as a possible guideline to others in communicating with top management:

Presumption: A major profit opportunity lies in the consolidation of the four Eastern plants into a new production facility at a new location of the company's own choosing.

Payback and costs: This was Item 1 on the agenda. Annual savings, payback, return on funds, and capital costs were estimated. The capital cost figures were arrived at by figuring the total cost of land, engineering, buildings, equipment, and contingency.

Present-plants analysis: The point was first made that none of the four present plants was at a site selected by the company. All of them had been extensively modified and expanded, but their locations were the result of business acquisition rather than careful site selection. They were old, and opportunity for their further expansion and modernization was limited. A table like the one shown in Exhibit 1 was drawn up to compare their age and size as well as their relative importance to the community. The original table also included the gross and net investment in each plant and

PRESENT LOCATION STATISTICS

	Hoboken	*Dorchester*	*Orange*	*LeRoy*
Age (years)	50	100+	75	65
Land (acres)	2	22	3	6
Buildings (square feet)	227M	582M	115M	136M
Employees	514	811	95	331
% Total community employment	2	*	10	23
% Total community tax	1	*	2	3

(*Less than 1 percent)

EXHIBIT 1

demonstrated that all four plants were well depreciated. Several points were raised in connection with this. First, over the years the company had made many additions and alterations at each plant. Second, attention was drawn to the fact that the total square footage was slightly over one million, which was spread over 40 buildings. This was 200,000 square feet more than was planned for the single new facility. Finally, the company's share of all the real and personal property taxes collected by the communities revealed that the towns of Orange and LeRoy might be seriously affected by a shutdown.

New facility timetable: A chart showing the proposed timing of shutdown and startup is reproduced in Exhibit 2. GF's fiscal year, it will be noted, begins in April. Several points were made in connection with this chart. The assumption was that the plants at Hoboken, Orange, and LeRoy would be vacated by March 1964. In computing the effect on profits, a further assumption was made that all three plants would be sold in March 1965 and that the loss on disposal would occur in the fiscal year 1964-1965. This was 13 months after the plants would be available for occupancy. The shaded lines in the chart indicated that the plants could be offered for sale as early as July 1963, with occupancy in March 1964. The assumption was that the Dorchester plant would be disposed of in March 1966. Idle plant expense, including depreciation, would be directly affected by the actual disposal dates, with favorable or unfavorable effect on profits depending upon actual plant sales.

The report was reinforced with detailed "reasons why" the proposed time schedule for engineering, construction, relocation, and startup was both realistic and obtainable. "The potential savings are so attractive

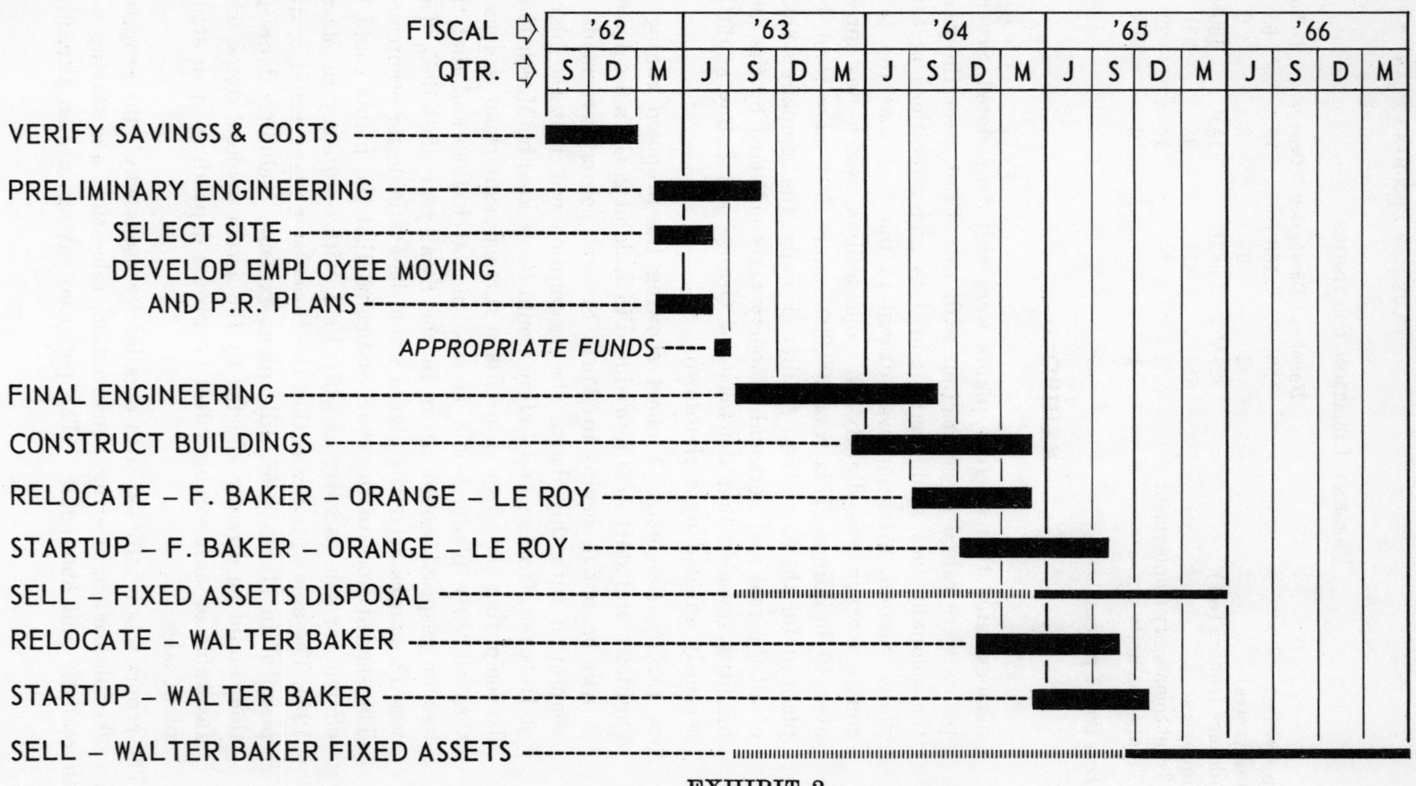
FISCAL
'62
'63
'64
'65
'66
QTR.
S D M J S D M J S D M J S D M J S D M
VERIFY SAVINGS & COSTS
PRELIMINARY ENGINEERING
SELECT SITE
DEVELOP EMPLOYEE MOVING
AND P.R. PLANS
APPROPRIATE FUNDS
FINAL ENGINEERING
CONSTRUCT BUILDINGS
RELOCATE – F. BAKER – ORANGE – LE ROY
STARTUP – F. BAKER – ORANGE – LE ROY
SELL – FIXED ASSETS DISPOSAL
RELOCATE – WALTER BAKER
STARTUP – WALTER BAKER
SELL – WALTER BAKER FIXED ASSETS

EXHIBIT 2

that we have a powerful incentive for proceeding as rapidly as possible,'' was the way the report stated it. ''Any delays to the timetable will place a severe financial penalty upon the company.'' In support of its position, the report listed the following categories of savings at the new plant:

1. Property taxes. The expectation was that real estate and other taxes would be lower at the new plant, and that there would be no inventory taxes.
2. Utilities. Lower rates for electric power, gas, and water were expected.
3. Labor rates and insurance. Wage rates were expected to be lower, as were workmen's compensation and unemployment insurance.
4. Bulk materials handling. The new facility was expected to have a complete system for the bulk handling of materials, plus grinding and grading facilities for sugar which would allow the purchase of a single grade rather than the five grades being used in the existing plants.
5. Direct labor and benefits. With all operations under one roof, fewer production workers would be required than in the existing plants, where operations were spread over 40 different buildings.
6. Indirect labor and benefits. The consolidation of activities from four plants into one offered enormous savings in the requirements for maintenance and warehouse workers and utility and service employees, as well as in such functions as quality control, personnel, purchasing, financial control, and engineering. For example, maintenance had 257 employees in the four old plants as against a planned 156 for the new plant; personnel had 34 as against a planned 18. Exhibit 3 compares the numbers of employees in the old and new plants.

Each of these categories was supported with dollar estimates of savings which added up to such an impressive total that an early—and favorable—decision from management seemed imperative.

Of course, the report also included data on the expense of consolidation. These were presented in six categories:

1. Transfers and terminations. Approximately 1,800 employees were involved. Average termination and moving costs were developed for both hourly and salaried personnel.
2. Start-up costs. This item included low initial operating efficiencies, materials losses, training costs, inventory buildups, employee bonuses for staying at the old plants until they closed, and some

Number of Employees—Present Versus Proposed

	Present	*New*	*Difference*
Management Personnel	88	85	– 3
Weekly salaried	549	369	–180
Hourly	1159	833	–326
Totals	1796	1287	–509

EXHIBIT 3

unavoidable duplication of effort during the shutdown and start-up period.

3. Expense on capital. This covered the removal, shipping, and reinstallation of equipment.
4. Retirement rebate. This was a credit item representing the recapture of company retirement fund contributions from terminated employees who had been in the retirement plan less than ten years.
5. Idle plant expense. This included depreciation, taxes, insurance, utilities, watchman services, and so forth.
6. Loss on fixed assets. This included the anticipated loss involved in the disposal of land, buildings, and nontransferable equipment at the four old plants.

The presentation to the operating policy committee was not entirely made up of figures on costs, savings, and profits. It also included reference to the attitude of the Jell-O Division with respect to the affected employees and the four old plant communities.

"Figures and statistics are cold and unemotional," the report said, "and the charts cannot convey to you the very deep concern we feel for the 1,800 employees in our four Eastern plants, all of whom would be affected by the proposed move. It is our determination to be fair, considerate, and sympathetic with each employee in the best GF tradition. This conviction does not show on the charts, but all of us have it."

The report pointed out that almost one-half of the 1,796 employees at the four old plants were 46 years of age or older—in other words, senior employees. Many had never worked for any other company; 314 had more than 25 years of service; 891 were in the 10-to-25-year bracket; 591 had been with GF less than 10 years.

Although the company had previous experience in closing plants and transferring personnel (see pages 101-102, Chapter VI) no move had been of the magnitude now contemplated, and there was little to suggest how many might transfer to a consolidated Eastern plant. Certainly, there was going to be a need for old and experienced employees in getting the new plant under way. There was, however, full realization that many of these old-timers had very strong family and community ties which would make them reluctant to move.

As for the four plant communities, it was obvious that LeRoy and Orange would be the harder hit by the shutdown of the old plants. "Obviously," the report said, "if we are able to sell the vacated plants to another business that can hire most of our terminated employees, the blow will be greatly softened." As for the effect on the new community, Jell-O saw this as being nothing but favorable and providing a clear opportunity for the company to earn the respect of the community for management, the new plant, and the employees.

After another brief summary of the possibilities for improving the four old plants, the report came to the following conclusion:

> After consideration of the adverse effect the proposed move will have on GF's profits for Fiscal 1964 and 1965, as well as the adverse effect on the present employees and the communities of LeRoy and Orange, the Jell-O Division believes that the profit improvement and provision for future growth to be derived from a new Eastern plant justifies the large capital expenditure. If management agrees with the foregoing, we recommend that funds be authorized now for preliminary engineering and site selection; that employee announcements and public relations plans be developed; and that capital funds for the new facility be appropriated by midsummer of 1962.

These were the salient features of the presentation made to the operating policy committee in February 1962 and to the board of directors on March 7, 1962. The board agreed with the conclusion. Employees and the press were informed immediately, even though the relocation site had not yet been selected. The idea was now a full-fledged plan, and it was time to begin a serious search for a plant site.

SELECTING THE SITE

Chapter III

SELECTING THE SITE

Selecting the site for the proposed new plant was a major concern, since significant savings would be involved in such expenses as transportation, taxes, utility costs, wage rates, unemployment insurance, and construction costs, which vary from place to place. A preliminary location survey had been made by the facilities study group and corporate engineering. It covered 21 locations in eight Eastern states and pointed strongly to a city in the Philadelphia-Wilmington-Baltimore area. The study group emphasized, however, that a more detailed study might identify a location that was even more favorable.

This, GF decided, was a job for specialists. The task of conducting the detailed study was assigned to the Fantus Company, one of the top consulting firms on plant location in the United States. Fantus could put at GF's disposal a staff of 40 engineers and economists with vast experience in labor, taxes, freight rates, construction costs, water and power supplies, and so forth, plus a large store of facts and figures about dozens of communities in the company's area of interest.

The Fantus Company's first step was to obtain all possible facts about

General Foods and the nature of the Jell-O Division operations which would be located at the new plant. GF was asked to complete a detailed questionnaire which would give Fantus the information necessary to begin its search for a suitable site.

Fantus began its site search with several limiting factors in mind. The new plant had to be built within the range of the primary market served by the four old plants and, preferably, within 250 miles of New York City. It had to be near an adequate ocean port or ports, since large quantities of raw materials would come from overseas. It was necessary that it be near a sugar refinery, since sugar consumption was expected to be more than a half million pounds per day. And, of course, the new plant had to be in a community that would be receptive to that type of industry.

Fantus presented its report to General Foods on May 1, 1962. It, too, centered attention on the Philadelphia-Wilmington-Baltimore area and gave detailed figures and specific site recommendations. Philadelphia and Baltimore are large cities in the Northeastern "megalopolis" of the United States. They have correspondingly large labor pools and many major industries, and both have excellent transportation facilities and are major East Coast ports. Dover, Delaware, on the other hand, was a small city (population 7,250 at the time of the survey), which had relatively little industry. It depended heavily upon its position as a trading center for an extensive rural area, on one sizable industry (International Latex Corporation), state government offices, and a large U. S. Air Force base. Nevertheless, Fantus found cogent reasons for recommending that the proposed plant be located at Dover rather than in one of the urban areas.

The Fantus report to GF covered three important topics in its site recommendations:

1. A review of the geographically variable cost factors influencing choice of location, especially the range of potential variations.
2. A delineation of the areas considered and the reasons for their selection.
3. A comparison of geographically variable operating costs in present plants and in the considered locations.

In arriving at its recommendations, Fantus first studied outbound freight costs on finished goods and inbound costs on various raw materials. The outbound costs were important because GF pays the cost of shipping its products to customers around the country. The key consideration among the raw materials costs was sugar. In early stages of the study, Jell-O management had placed emphasis upon the possibility of inducing a sugar refinery to locate near the new plant; since this would require deep-water frontage, the study at first considered only waterfront locations. However, it developed that the sugar industry was not willing to establish an additional refinery on the East Coast and that the new plant would have to rely upon existing refineries located in Boston, New York, Philadelphia, and Baltimore. This substantially changed the basic geographic orientation of the search: a waterfront site was no longer necessary. But the new plant's projected requirement for sugar resulted in the GF decision that, if possible, the plant be within 10 miles and not beyond 50 miles of a sugar refinery.

Other needed raw materials—cocoa beans, coconut, and tapioca—also suggested a location oriented to a general merchandise port. Again, a waterfront site was studied, but the idea was rejected because individual cargoes were not always sufficiently large to justify discharge at a private dock. Potential savings did not appear sufficient to offset the larger capital outlay for waterfront facilities.

Next on the list of locational factors was labor availability and probable cost. Since the company's basic planning had included process flow charts, general plant arrangement layouts, and manning tables for the new plant, Fantus knew that total employment was estimated at 1,287 persons. In addition, the company had estimated—on the basis of early interviews with employees—that 439 persons would transfer from the four old plants to the new location. (This was obviously something of a "guesstimate," since at this juncture the company had not decided upon a new location. Employees knew only that the four old plants would be consolidated at some spot as yet unidentified. However, the estimate proved to be fairly close because 423 employees eventually made the move to Dover.) This meant that the new community would be called upon to furnish an estimated 848 employees who could meet the company's requirements.

Fantus was, of course, aware of a long-standing GF policy of paying wages and salaries consistent with local patterns. Accordingly, full consideration was given to various area wage and salary differentials and their relative stability. Fantus concluded, however, that it could not rely solely upon data from the Bureau of Labor Statistics which represented "Average Hourly Earnings of Production Workers," since these data included the entire "mix" of industry in each area.

More reliance could be placed upon a comparison of industry-by-industry averages, but even here some comparisons might be misleading.

For example, in Wilmington, where the chemical industry dominated local employment with 50.5 percent of all manufacturing employees, the higher chemical industry wage rates were more likely to be the controlling factor than the much lower rates in food industries, which represented only 4.3 percent of all industrial employment.

Fantus recommended that a detailed study of wage structures be made among leading local firms to provide the accuracy needed for comparison. Such surveys were made in Philadelphia, Baltimore, and Dover. Fantus did recommend ruling out one city in the area because of its high payroll costs.

One seemingly insurmountable problem was the transfer of employees from Franklin Baker Coconut in Hoboken and Walter Baker Chocolate in Dorchester—both relatively high-wage areas—into a community such as Dover, where the company would adopt the prevailing lower wage scales. However, a study of the problem showed that actual downward adjustments could be minor. The widest differentials were in the unskilled labor categories, while the company's estimate of transferees showed that most would be in the advanced-skill categories. In addition, adjustments could be minimized by offering promotions to qualified employees upon their transfer or, if necessary, by creating temporary "master" grades for key workers who were at or near the top of their classifications. Such special categories could be phased out of the picture as these workers were promoted or retired.

The Fantus analysis of construction costs showed that in general New England and New York tended to exceed the national average, while Philadelphia and Wilmington had costs near the average. Cities further south had lower construction costs.

Local taxes, according to the report, could not be considered until the study approached final site selection because of the wide variability in such taxation. Variations within states were frequently larger than those between states. However, it was decided to avoid any county or community which taxed personal property, since the new plant would have large investments in machinery, equipment, and inventory.

State income and franchise taxes also showed wide variations. When measured against similar taxes at the four old plants, the rates in various states showed a net effect for the company ranging from a saving of $473,000 per year up to a penalty of $443,000. The report warned, however, that no conclusions should be drawn in this matter unless the impact of local taxation was considered at the same time.

The report also pointed out the wide variations in premiums for workmen's compensation insurance. These ranged from $.75 per $100 of payroll in Delaware and Pennsylvania up to $2.35 in New Jersey. Fantus also warned that in some states the initial unemployment insurance rate would be determined by the favorable or unfavorable fund position occupied by existing GF installations. Actual rates ranged from 1.5 to 4.2 percent.

Fantus also took a hard look at utility costs in various cities throughout the area under consideration and reported on capacities and the reliability of service.

After considering all factors, Fantus summed up the survey information in the following conclusions:

1. Outbound freight costs will be minimized from sites in the vicinity of Philadelphia-Wilmington-Baltimore.
2. The unwillingness of the sugar industry to establish new facilities requires GF to locate this plant reasonably close to an existing refinery.
3. Heavy movement of other raw materials over piers suggests a location oriented to a general cargo port.
4. Combined freight costs favor the Philadelphia-Wilmington-Baltimore area.
5. The GF decision to maintain local wage and salary levels suggests potential selection of an outlying, low-cost community generally oriented to Philadelphia-Wilmington-Baltimore.
6. Combined state and local taxes are lowest in Delaware. Maryland is acceptable only if the county exempts personal property.
7. Construction costs will be lowest in southern portions of the area under consideration.

The report concluded with an estimate of operating cost savings for the three proposed plant sites in Philadelphia, Baltimore, and Dover. Delaware's capital city emerged as the definite winner because it offered the following unique advantages in addition to tax attractions:

1. Wage differentials have persisted for decades.
2. Most of the local industries, including International Latex (2,100 employees) and the canning plants, enjoyed good labor-management relationships.
3. Within a 30-mile radius the estimated supply of workers seeking industrial employment is 5,000 males and 3,000 females.
4. Living conditions are superior to those in typical cities in its class, reflecting the combined presence of the state offices, a college, and an Air Force installation.

5. Good freight transportation services are available, including an active line of the Pennsylvania Railroad.
6. Excellent sites served by rail and all utilities can be acquired at low cost.

Fantus specifically recommended one site of ample acreage which was bounded on one side by the railroad and had all utilities in place on another side. This property, which eventually became the site of the new plant, was not within Dover's city limits at the time. This caused some concern to GF management, since property outside the city was not subject to zoning regulations. At a later date, however, the area was annexed by the city.

The Fantus report by no means pictured Dover as being totally perfect as a site for the new plant. It also listed some potential problems as follows:

1. No skilled labor is available, and an extensive training program is envisioned.
2. Housing, though remarkably modern, is in short supply. Some GF aid may be necessary.
3. Upon completion of their 33,000-kilowatt municipal power plant, Dover officials canceled a power supply contract with the Delaware Power & Light Company. Negotiations will be necessary to insure service by the utility company.
4. Some surplus capacity is available in the water system and sewage treatment plant. Plans for their expansion should be expedited to correspond with GF construction schedules.

On the whole, however, Dover looked good to the Jell-O Division management. There seemed to be many advantages to locating there, only a few disadvantages, and some unanswered questions. Certainly a closer look at the community was indicated, but obviously this could not be had without disclosing that Dover was under serious consideration as the site for the new plant. So on May 15, 1962, the Jell-O Division general manager notified all employees at the four old plants that Dover was "one of the leading sites under consideration" and that the company had an option to purchase 115 acres of land. At the same time company officials set up a meeting in Delaware with state and city officials and issued a press release revealing that land had been optioned at Dover.

Dover's reaction to this announcement was understandably enthusiastic. What small city wouldn't be overjoyed at being told it was the current number-one choice as the location for a plant of the type GF intended to build? As one newspaper editorial pointed out, "General Foods' plan has the kind of built-in appeal that produces an enthusiastic community response: It will employ a relatively high number of people; it isn't likely to offend the eyes, the ears, or the noses of its neighbors. . . ."

The response of state and city officials and the press seemed to be dimmed but little by the company's statement that "several fundamental questions remain to be settled before a decision can be reached to build in this area and on this particular site." Most of these questions concerned the city's willingness and ability to provide the necessary utility services and zoning protection. Dover's mayor pledged the city to "do everything possible to meet the needs," while the press said it had "no doubts" that all requirements could be met.

In addition to information about utilities and zoning, management also wanted to get a more definitive fix on the Dover area labor pool, particularly in the skilled-craft categories. GF decided, therefore, to backstop the findings of the Fantus report with a survey of Dover which could at the same time give management a better overall picture of the community. Accordingly, in June 1962 the company retained Douglas Williams Associates of New York City, survey research specialists, to make a Dover community study to determine the following:

1. What are the attitudes and feelings of people in the area that bear on whether General Foods should locate there? More specifically, would people in the area be desirous of working in the plant? What are the work characteristics of the employable people? Would the company be welcomed as a new neighbor? What is the status of race relations? What are the union attitudes in the community?
2. What is the availability of skilled-craft labor? How many such men live in the area? How skilled are they? Would they be interested in working for Jell-O?

Dover officials were informed of the forthcoming survey. However, in the interest of keeping the findings as objective as possible, GF suggested a minimum of press coverage. Newspapers carried only a brief, one-paragraph announcement.

The Williams survey was run in three parts. To begin with, three senior staff members from Douglas Williams talked with 35 community leaders. Included in the group were educators; men prominent in business, government, and the law; members of the clergy; press and radio representatives; and heads of community associations and clubs.

As the second step, personal interviews by the questionnaire method were conducted with 304 adult residents of the area. Forty-four of the 304 interviews were with Negroes—this being consistent with census figures showing the area to have a 15 percent colored population—and these interviews were conducted by a Negro.

The third part of the survey was conducted by four senior interviewers, all knowledgeable in the skills required in plant work. They interviewed 43 men identified as skilled craftsmen in order to learn how experienced they were, to get an understanding of the probable level of their skill, and to see how interested they might be in working in the new plant.

The interviews with community leaders brought out a strong and persistent theme: ''We want General Foods.'' The flavor of this sentiment, according to the Williams report, was not that of a planned Chamber of Commerce promotion: ''Individuals spoke as individuals, each reflecting his own attitude. The desire of the town's leaders to have General Foods seems to be unanimous.''

Negative points, according to the report, were notable by their absence and were always referred to as something someone else said and not something the person himself believed. The following points were brought up only once or twice each:

1. The arrival of the GF plant might cause wage rates to increase in the whole area.
2. The plant will take farm lands out of production.
3. ''Old Doverites'' might be against it (an old guard found in many communities who want the town's historical traditions maintained and no changes made).
4. The plant might cause a nuisance (odor, stream pollution).
5. The plant might use an excessive amount of water.

None of these points, as it later turned out, was the subject of any significant number of complaints during the plant's first two years of operation. They are included here as an example of negative aspects which others might find more significant under different circumstances.

The subject of racial relations was of concern to GF since it had been an equal-opportunity employer since 1937. Would there be resistance to this policy in the Dover area? Williams' interviewers found that the desegregation process in Dover was proceeding quite smoothly, even though much of it was still on a token basis. Negro leaders felt that the pace was about all that could be expected and were pleased with the fact that school integration had begun. Among the community leaders, the interviewers found two types of people, both of whom regarded the process as inevitable. ''One group doesn't mind it,'' the report stated. ''The other group, while recognizing increasing integration as an accomplished fact, resents it to the marrow. Deeper, in fact.''

Williams found, however, a ''recurring theme,'' so to speak, and that was that GF could follow its own wishes with respect to integration; that the important point was to declare its policy firmly at the start and then stick to it.

In questioning key people on their attitudes regarding labor unions, Williams found little to suggest that this would be an issue: ''These men don't like the concept of labor unions, but there has been so little experience with them in the area that they don't think much about the subject.''

In each discussion with these people, the interviewers posed a question like this: ''If a company like General Foods came to Dover, what are some of the things it should do, or should not do, to get off to a good start?'' They found a ''high degree of uniformity in response to this, and always on a serious note. Usually people said, in one way or another, 'Don't push.' It would be important for Jell-O and Jell-O people to be willing to participate. That is clear. But apparently one should wait until one is asked, rather than stepping forth on his own recognizance.''

After talking with Dover's community leaders, the interviewers set out to question 304 residents of the area, who were selected at random. Again, they found many plus factors.

The respondents were overwhelmingly in favor of having GF move to Dover. Ninety-four percent wanted the plant, and 93 percent agreed that the area would be a better place if the new industry moved in. Ninety percent thought that the new plant would be a good place in which to work, and a third of the respondents felt that they or some member of their families would want to have a job there. They were mostly interested in factory or construction work, but a goodly number expressed interest in white-collar jobs; only a few were interested in skilled-craft and management-level positions. The questionnaires revealed that 270 of the 304 respondents were employed or employable and that there were an additional 215 such persons in their immediate households.

On the matter of integration, the report stated: ''There was definite resistance to integration. Among the whites queried, only 20 percent thought integration a good thing. Forty percent said 'no,' leaving 30 percent with qualified answers. Attitudes toward labor unions were pretty well split, although less than one-third were definitely in favor of employees being unionized.''

Perhaps the most important phase of the report had to do with the skilled-craft situation. The evidence suggested that there were a good many skilled workers, some of whom seemed to have the necessary qualifications to work at GF. Moreover, many of them planned to apply at the new Jell-O Division plant. The feeling was that additional skilled labor could be recruited from surrounding counties. Of particular importance, also, was the finding that both the State Vocational Training Department and a local junior college had offered their services in helping the Jell-O people develop training programs. The Williams report summed up the situation as follows: ''The advantages of a loyal work force, which is stable and productive, are so great, and the indications are that this can be achieved in Dover, that the effort should be on seeing how the necessary skilled craft people can be obtained for there.''

Regarding the community attitude, the report stated: ''It is normal for community studies of this nature to present a somewhat mixed picture—a ledger made up of assets and liabilities. In Dover, however, community sentiment seems to come out totally on the asset side.''

Thus GF now had two reports agreeing that Dover was the best site for the proposed plant. Nevertheless, the time for decision was not yet at hand. Still to be resolved were many problems concerning the plant's requirements for electric power, water, sewers, and zoning protection; it was to be almost four months before GF finally gave the nod to Dover.

Company engineers had been discussing the problems of utilities and zoning with city officials since the announcement in May 1962 that Dover was under consideration as the plant site.

With respect to electric power, Dover had the recently completed 33,000-kilowatt power plant and the canceled tie-in agreement with a private firm, Delaware Power & Light. GF asked that some sort of tie-in be reinstated to provide a dual power source as a guarantee against interruptions in service. An agreement was eventually reached to tie the plant directly to Delaware Power & Light facilities, but with the city selling the power to GF.

Then there was the question of sewers and water facilities. The city's existing sewage treatment plant appeared to be inadequate to handle the expected plant wastes. However, some improvement and expansion of the plant had already been planned to handle extensions of the city sewage system. Furthermore, the city had under consideration the construction of a secondary treatment plant. City officials agreed to speed up both projects. The water system was also expanded to meet the needs of the plant.

Regarding zoning, the city had regulations, but the county did not. Thus GF's proposed site, which was outside the city limits, was unprotected. In August 1962 the city attempted through a referendum to annex a large area that included the proposed plant site. The referendum failed. However, city officials moved immediately to get "letters of intent" from owners of several farms near the site, and a sufficiently large area was eventually annexed.

The final decision to move to Dover was made at a meeting of GF's board of directors on September 5, 1962. An immediate announcement was made to employees at the affected plants, to state and city officials at Dover, and to the press. Dover was jubilant. "This," wrote the editor of the local paper, "is the greatest thing that ever happened to Dover."

The long search for a site was over. It had been a thorough search, conducted by experts, and with good results. GF liked Dover, and it appeared that Dover liked GF. Two years later the company is more than ever able to say with all sincerity: "We're glad we came to Dover."

DESIGNING, ENGINEERING, AND BUILDING THE NEW PLANT

Chapter IV

DESIGNING, ENGINEERING, AND BUILDING THE NEW PLANT

The "go ahead" from GF's board of directors on March 7, 1962, had cleared the way and provided the money for Phase III—preliminary engineering. The studies by the task force, by Jell-O's facilities improvement group, and by corporate manufacturing and engineering had made it obvious that designing, engineering, and building the proposed new plant was going to be a tremendous task—the biggest GF had ever undertaken—and the preliminary engineering was one of the important phases.

Thus even before board approval of the plan to consolidate the four Eastern plants, corporate manufacturing and engineering had outlined the objective of Phase III and listed the tasks to be performed by each participant. From an engineering point of view, the overall objective was:

A. To determine product allocation, plant site, engineering data, and flow charts in sufficient detail to permit the planning, engineering, construction, and equipping of a new Jell-O and chocolate processing and packaging plant having a capacity to process the products at the sales volume level anticipated in the peak quarter of Fiscal 1968.

B. To perform the planning and engineering necessary to construct and equip a warehouse having a capacity capable of storing packaged raw materials, packing materials, and finished goods required to support the anticipated sales volume level in Fiscal 1970.

The immediate objective was to develop the preliminary engineering and design for the Jell-O and chocolate processing and packaging plant, warehouse, office, and auxiliary buildings.

The Jell-O Division, the manufacturing and engineering director, and the project manager for engineering design and construction divided the engineering assignments in the following way:

1. *Jell-O Division will:*
   a. Provide continuous guidance, consultation, and review throughout this phase of the project.
   b. Provide all information needed, such as sales forecasts, formulas, operating procedures, and so forth.
   c. Provide research as needed to determine if proposed processes or equipment will be satisfactory and develop processes and equipment, materials, and whatever else needed.
2. *Manufacturing and Engineering Director will:*
   a. Review all aspects of this phase of the project in the general corporate interest.
3. *Engineering Design and Construction will:*
   a. Prepare preliminary flow sheets showing various possibilities of handling the different products.
   b. Present flow sheets for discussion.
   c. Obtain approval on acceptable sheets noting all processes and equipment to be evaluated and developed.
   d. Evaluate and develop all processes and equipment.
   e. Present revised flow sheets for discussion indicating state of evaluation.
   f. Revise flow sheets and present for final approval and signature.
   g. Investigate airveying of sugar and handling of one grade of sugar.
   h. Prepare detailed list of new and old equipment.
   i. Obtain detailed information on all old equipment.
   j. Obtain data on new equipment.

k. Prepare preliminary equipment layout for discussion purposes—layouts to be based on flow sheets and minimum manpower requirements.
l. Use data obtained in discussions to revise layouts for final approval.
m. Make an analysis of typical building construction for sanitation and cost.
n. Develop building sections.
o. Develop finished schedules.
p. Size buildings based on equipment layouts.
q. Prepare model showing entire plant with its equipment.

4. *Special Projects will:*
   a. In cooperation with outside consultants, do site selection work.
   b. Basing them on sales forecast by district for peak quarter of Fiscal 1968, allocate products for the new facility.
   c. In cooperation with outside consultants, develop a critical path schedule.
5. *Industrial Engineering will:*
   a. Using the product allocation made by Special Projects, determine peak quarter requirements, pack sizes, and technical specifications for the manufacture of each item.
   b. Identify sequence of manufacture where one phase of equipment might be used in the production run of several different items.
   c. Develop preliminary requirements for raw materials and in-process materials, basing them on finished goods requirements and anticipated materials shrinkage and technical or safety requirements.
   d. Develop inventory levels as defined by the COPT System and the warehouse requirements necessary to house these inventories. This analysis is to include all bulk and packaged items.
   e. Make economic analysis on major equipment costs where the choice of two or more systems exists.
   f. Prepare make-or-buy analysis.
   g. Identify the preliminary cost reductions resulting from introduction of new processes, equipment, or other source.
   h. Analyze the basic materials flow requirements, assist with the layout analysis, and make recommendations.
   i. Define the preliminary stores items inventory level, storage space and equipment requirements, layout and labor requirements.
   j. Define the preliminary requirements for the maintenance activity to include: equipment, space, layout, and manpower by job classification.
   k. Develop the preliminary materials handling equipment requirements and specifications for the warehouse, plant areas, and maintenance shops.

l. Develop manpower requirements for all functions reporting to the Manager of Manufacturing and Engineering, including all salaried and hourly rated jobs of direct and indirect classification.

m. Develop service area requirements in the plant for locker rooms, toilets, lunch rooms, plant offices, and so forth.

Corporate manufacturing and engineering, faced with the prospect of having the primary responsibility for the engineering and construction of the new plant, knew it could not perform this task with its normal staff. Fortunately, it had been using outside architectural-engineering consultants for many years and had kept files of all inquiries from such firms to GF. Thus its initial search for outside assistance began with a review of the more than 150 firms listed in its files.

On the basis of size, location, and experience, the list was quickly reduced to 20 such firms. With respect to size, corporate manufacturing and engineering felt that the firm should have available a staff of at least 150 architects and engineers—and preferably more—so that the Jell-O plant would not comprise too large a percentage of the firm's total workload. Location was not an excluding factor per se, but it was obvious that considerable additional time and expense would be incurred if the work was contracted to a company a great distance away from GF's headquarters at White Plains and the Technical Center at Tarrytown, New York.

Some firms, even though located in New York City, were dropped from consideration because of lack of experience in industrial work. In the final analysis, it was found that the most experienced firms in the industrial-process field were engineer-contractor combinations, and the list of 20 was largely made up of this type of firm.

Representatives of each of the 20 firms were interviewed after having been given some concept of the job they would be required to do. Each was requested to submit a complete proposal for preliminary engineering and a general outline of the manner in which it would perform the work. All firms were told that only the preliminary engineering was involved at that time but that the successful firm would be given every consideration for the final engineering phase and, in the case of the engineer-contractors, for the construction as well.

The firm finally selected to assist with the preliminary engineering—and ultimately to do the final engineering and construction—was the Bechtel Corporation, which had its headquarters in San Francisco but maintained a well-staffed and well-equipped office in New York City.

Bechtel was one of the country's leading engineer-contractor firms, with considerable experience in process engineering — particularly in the petroleum and chemical fields—and in the design and construction of industrial plants. It had some experience in the food and food-related industries but nothing on the scale envisioned for the Dover plant.

Work was already under way on the preparation of the flow sheets for all the processing and packaging lines included in the four old plants. Plant managers were asked to supply detailed lists of all old equipment as well as suggested new equipment. However, the basic concept was to move existing equipment for all processes from the four old plants to Dover. Preliminary equipment layouts were to be prepared based upon the flow sheets and minimum manpower requirements. From these, the size of various sections of the building could be determined.

It was at once apparent that the new plant would be highly complex. Any one process—except for chocolate processing—was fairly simple, but when added together they required a plant capable of performing dry mixing, wet mixing, spray drying, cooking, steaming, belt drying, many conveying methods, many types of packaging, and so forth. In the grocery line, the plant would produce about 75 products in some 135 packs. Added to this were 350 industrial products in more than 500 packs.

Bechtel's engineers employed two relatively new techniques during the preliminary engineering stage. One was the use of the critical path method to develop a project timetable; the other was the extensive use of block models to establish the final plant and equipment layout.

The critical path method requires that all of the individual steps and activities in the project be identified and time requirements estimated for each. After this is done, all steps are diagrammed so that the longest path—that is, the sequence of longest steps—determines total project time requirements and the proper sequence of steps wherein a delay in any one step would result in delaying the entire project. The Dover project involved so many factors that a computer was employed to determine the critical path layout.

The block models were based upon the flow sheets and preliminary equipment layouts.* Blocks were scaled to actual equipment dimensions and placed in production-line sequences. The model could then be manipulated and oriented to achieve an optimum arrangement. Production

*See Armstrong, Richard, "Precision Scale Models Replace Engineering Drawings," *Food Processing*, February 1965.

engineers studied the model from the standpoint of materials handling and processing requirements. Industrial engineers looked at floor space; manpower requirements; and the location of rail sidings, truck docks, raw material storage facilities, and warehousing. Maintenance engineers checked on the location of shops and repair facilities with respect to critical equipment, and quality control personnel checked on the location of laboratories with respect to production lines from which frequent samples had to be taken. However, what was perhaps the most valuable check was made by foremen and experienced production personnel, who looked at the models from a practical operational point of view in an attempt to identify various problem areas. The final layout of the models was incorporated into layout drawings, which were used during actual construction.

At a later date Bechtel engineers made precision scale models of two of the more complex areas of the Dover plant—the spray-drying towers and a large cocoa bean roaster. These precision models were exact miniatures of the complete processing systems with every piece of equipment —tanks, pumps, valves, piping, ducts—all in place. These models were constructed in the same manner and sequence as the full-scale equipment in the plant: floors were built; equipment was put in place; piping, pumps, and valves were connected; clearances were checked and interferences eliminated. When the models were completed and approved, detailed photographs were taken from all angles and construction drawings were made. The finished models, photos, and drawings were all sent to the building site for reference during construction.

Although the precision scale models were expensive and time consuming to build, they proved to be extremely valuable aids, not only during construction but also at a later date in training personnel who would work in those areas of the plant. The time required to build the models was offset to some extent by time saved through the elimination of numerous detailed engineering drawings, and the cost of the models was offset by a significant reduction in last minute changes after construction had started.

Bechtel and corporate manufacturing and engineering completed Phase III—preliminary engineering—in September 1962, and GF's board of directors authorized the largest capital appropriation in the company's history for construction of the new plant. Construction began on October 18, 1962, after appropriate ground-breaking ceremonies. At this stage only 10 percent of the final engineering had been completed. Thus construction and engineering were done simultaneously during most of the project. In fact, final engineering was not completed until several months after the plant had begun limited production on certain lines.

One may well question the advisability of starting construction on the basis of such a limited amount of the final engineering. However, management had carefully weighed the advantages and disadvantages before giving the word to go ahead and had decided that the potential gains outweighed the obvious risks. The advantages were as follows:

1. Earlier realization of cost savings and increased profits.
2. Earlier opportunity to do much-needed expansion of spray-drying facilities.
3. The opportunity to install new equipment for several other processes and to do it in a permanent place.
4. Lower engineering and construction overhead costs.
5. Faster elimination of the problems inherent in the four old plants.

The disadvantages encountered in such a procedure were as follows:

1. A high degree of risk in estimating costs and scheduling construction and production so as to avoid out-of-stock situations.
2. Inefficiencies caused by the necessity of making changes after construction was under way.
3. Higher enginering costs and more cost-plus-fee work by the contractor.
4. More difficulties in cost control with resulting higher costs of accounting.

In retrospect, it is evident that management made a sound decision in authorizing construction at a time when there was only a very general definition of the size and scope of the project. Waiting for the completion of engineering would have delayed the project nearly a year, with the resulting loss of profit stemming both from cost savings at the new plant and the more rapid production of certain new and profitable products.

This is not to say that there were no difficulties caused by the early start of construction. Actually, most of the disadvantages listed above were encountered; however, they were considerably outweighed by the advantages.

Construction of the plant and installation of equipment was a massive undertaking—"the most complex and complicated job we ever did," according to one Bechtel official. Nevertheless, once under way, the job moved ahead rapidly, though not without some inevitable delay.

The principal engineering and construction delays can be traced to the following factors:

1. The beginning of construction with only a small percentage of final engineering completed, which made it necessary on occasion for construction to wait for the completion of engineering.
2. GF's understandable desire to incorporate many changes in the new plant even though the project was originally planned on the basis of simply moving the four old plants to one location. Actually, almost everyone connected with the project saw the new plant as providing a magnificent opportunity to introduce process improvements, new equipment, a certain amount of automation, and so forth. In addition, it sometimes proved to be physically impossible to install old production lines from the multi-storied plants in the modern one-story building. Naturally, many of these changes required lengthy engineering and cost studies which sometimes delayed their introduction into the project and caused some portions of the construction to be held up.
3. Inability to "freeze" the state of the business. As construction of the plant went forward, so did research and development on new products, new packages, and new processes. There were sales projection changes, new marketing plans, and so on. This caused requirements for processing equipment and packaging machinery to change almost continuously.
4. The addition of several millions of dollars in separately authorized projects for new products on top of an already complicated combination of processing and packaging lines. Many of these were approved after substantial engineering had been completed in the affected areas. One major addition required alterations to the completed building structure and to the utility system.

Among the other possible factors was the fact that many of the contractor's supervisory people did not have knowledge of food plant standards or specific experience in food plant construction. Moreover, experienced packaging-equipment people were in short supply; there were frequent changes of key field personnel; and occasionally there was inadequate checking of subcontractor performance.

For a time, a major problem was the division of responsibility between Jell-O and the corporate engineering department, in that the contractor was often confused about approvals of work to be done, changes, additions, deletions, and so forth. There was also an apparent division of responsibility between Bechtel's offices in New York and San Francisco: GF people were not always sure where to seek answers to their questions. Nearly all who were directly connected with the construction of the Dover plant are convinced of the desirability—or even the absolute necessity—of having a single center of responsibility on the part of both the company and the engineer-contractor.

Although there are several existing records of the construction project, the details are not included here since other such projects would undoubtedly be concerned with vastly different types of plants and the history of this one would not be a useful guide. The following brief highlights from the contractor's monthly reports to GF serve to indicate how the project progressed:

October 1962—Final engineering under way . . . architectural plans being prepared . . . work started on final arrangements of preliminary models.

November 1962—Engineering activity concentrated on critical construction items and equipment with long lead time . . . some model arrangements completed . . . site being prepared . . . overall project schedule submitted to GF.

December 1962—Major project controls prepared—drawing controls, specification controls, new and relocated equipment summaries, and requisition controls.

January 1963—Engineering fell behind schedule because of continued shifting layouts, revised equipment selection and process flows, changes in design criteria, etc.

February 1963—Engineering manpower increased to 200 . . . introduced a "want list" for design criteria needed to complete engineering.

March 1963—Engineering 45 percent complete . . . force at site averaged 344 . . . many gaps in dimensional information due to lack of vendor drawings.

April 1963—Began planning of equipment relocation.

May 1963—Engineering 71 percent complete . . . force at site increased to 600.

June 1963—Force at site increased to 800 . . . increasing indications of probable delays in startup.

July 1963—Engineering 85 percent complete . . . field force up to 950.

August 1963—Field force 1,280.

September 1963—Experiencing delivery problems with subcontractors and suppliers . . . field force 1,325.

October 1963—First move of equipment from Dorchester under way . . . field force 1,728.

November 1963—First Hoboken move under way . . . first cocoa beans placed in silos . . . appointed corporate engineering relocation manager and counterpart for Bechtel who were responsible for coordinating all moves of existing equipment and installation for incremental startups.

December 1963—Equipment moves begun from LeRoy.

January 1964—Dorchester move rescheduled from two phases to three.

March 1964—Uncertain scope of start-up modifications created a problem in forecasting costs.

April 1964—Engineering closed out at Bechtel's New York office.

May 1964—All engineering work on basic project complete.

September 1964—All relocation of equipment essentially complete.

October 1964—All work on basic project complete.

Even under the most favorable estimating conditions there were bound to be unforeseeables of major significance in an engineering undertaking as vast and complex as the Dover move. And in this particular case, when the original estimate and appropriation were made on the basis of 10 percent of the engineering, some miscalculation was almost inevitable.

The following is the way the operations manager of the Jell-O Division put the matter to the operating policy committee on August 16, 1963, under four separate but interrelated categories.

Timetable: Jell-O/Dover has experienced a number of minor delays but none serious enough to jeopardize the start-up schedule as planned. All four of the plant shutdowns are coming along within the timetable earlier presented. There has been some compression of moving, installation, and start-up activities, with a corresponding loss of flexibility and increase in risk.

Project Costs: It must be remembered that 65 percent of the current cost forecast is based on costs to date, firm commitments, and estimates from final engineering drawings and specifications. Thirty-five percent is based on partially completed engineering, including parts of the more difficult areas to estimate, such as electrical work, piping, equipment-installation details, used-equipment relocation, and plant start-up costs. At the same time, cost reductions have been made in many areas through division and engineering studies and have helped to offset additions. Opportunities for further capital cost reductions are not as great now as in the earlier stages of the job. We must continue close cost and schedule control of engineering commitments and construction. *In being realistic about the problems that we will face in final engineering and plant operation, we must recognize that there is a possibility of exceeding the original capital appropriation.* By mid-November 1963, when the engineering will be about 95 percent completed and expenditures and commitments at about 50 percent of the anticipated total, and we are still ten months away from substantial completion of the project, we will be able to produce a new, realistic, detailed accounting.

One-Time Expenses: This category is separately financed and is directly chargeable to the Jell-O Division under prevailing corporate accounting policies. It includes employee moving and termination, employee training, equipment reconditioning and transfer, start-up costs such as labor and materials, inventory build-up costs, and loss on the sale of the four old plants. A review of these expenses indicates that we are on plan in total as well as by the breakdown in terms of fiscal years.

Savings and Payback: The Dover project was authorized on the basis of an average annual saving of several million dollars. A review of our savings estimate shows an increase of $0.2 million due to wage and salary escalation. The payback and return will improve slightly over the authorization request of August 20, 1962, if the project costs no more than the original estimate.

Summary: We are not yet prepared to say that the move schedule, capital costs, or one-time expense estimates must be revised upward. It is apparent, however, that we have used a relatively large part of our "float" time, thus reducing our ability to absorb delays without changing the move schedule; also, we have used a relatively large part of our project contingency fund, thus reducing our ability to absorb added costs without requesting a supplement to the capital project. By mid-November we will be in a much better position to know whether it will be necessary to request a supplement and, if so, in what amount.

Thus the groundwork was laid for making, in the spring of 1964, a formal request for supplemental capital funds with which to complete the Dover project. As the Jell-O operations manager described the situation:

> We all underestimated the magnitude and the complexity of the job. By late 1963 it was evident that the dynamics of the food processing industry would inevitably involve the Dover plant in an expansion of activity to a much greater extent than had been envisioned for it at the time the original appropriation request had been submitted.

As the time approached when Jell-O would shape up its request for supplemental capital funds, depth studies were conducted in every phase of the operation. Engineers, both within the organization and from Bechtel, were called upon for fresh appraisals. Experts in every related field contributed new estimates based upon the unfolding dynamics of the industry. There could be no second-guessing from that point on in.

When a draft of the revised estimate had been prepared, the Jell-O operations manager prepared a list of every question that might be raised and set down the answers. This was not only an exercise in self-discipline but also a way to insure that everyone involved would learn all there was to be learned about the project prior to the request for additional funds.

The questions and answers constitute a comprehensive picture of the dilemma and are reproduced here for their possible usefulness to others confronted with the need to go to the board, hat in hand, for further financing:

Q. Is the scope of the project now clearly defined?
A. Yes, engineering is virtually complete. All of the 1,428 drawings for the project have been completed. Buildings and utilities are complete.

Q. Was there any allowance for unknowns or omissions in the original estimate?
A. Yes—a contingency of several million was included to cover unknown items.

Q. Why wasn't more allowance made for unforeseeables in the original request when it was known that engineering was only 10 percent complete?
A. There was a failure in interpreting this preliminary engineering knowledge into a cost estimate. This "communication gap" was not identified until final engineering was well under way. The allowance for unknowns was not projected properly to cover the scope of this project.

Q. How much contingency allowance is included in the supplemental request?

A. Contingency for unknown items and modifications is approximately $1 million, over and above completion of identified installation details and allowance for start-up modifications or rearrangement.

Q. Is this enough to cover all the unknowns that lie ahead?

A. Yes, in sufficient amount to make all phases of the plan operational and complete based on projected products and volumes.

Q. What assurance is there the project can be completed within the supplement?

A. Engineering is now complete; buildings and services are essentially complete; and after a careful review of equipment start-up experience to date, Bechtel, Corporate Engineering, and Jell-O agree on the balance of work to be done. The present cost estimate reflects this work, and there is a high degree of assurance that the project can be completed within the supplemental request.

Q. Are start-up costs included in the capital request?

A. Start-up costs pertaining to equipment modifications and process changes to complete the project scope are included in the project. Start-up costs for labor, materials, and efficiency losses have been projected as a one-time expense item.

Q. What is the experience to date with respect to start-up costs?

A. Experience to date indicates that start-up costs with respect to labor and efficiency losses are in line with previous plans. Nine packing lines are in operation out of a total of 61.

Q. Is Bechtel building a good plant?

A. Yes.

Q. Can Dover be considered the ultimate in food-plant design and construction?

A. Jell-O/Dover is a modern, well-laid-out plant that lends itself well to flexibility and expansion, that will be easy to maintain. The processes are the same in principle as in the old plants, with better layout and flow.

Q. Has there been an area of extravagance in the buildings or equipment?

A. No. The plant, equipment, and process conditions provided are those necessary to meet the requirements of the products and their characteristics, to meet sanitary requirements and minimize costs.

Q. Was the experience gained from earlier GF projects used in estimating the complexity and cost of the Dover project?

A. Yes, but GF had no comparable experience of the dimensions of Dover. The supplemental need is due to underestimating space and utility requirements rather than improper pricing. Urgency to complete, to obtain early and substantial profit, made early authorization more important.

Q. How could the building-cost portion of the project be missed by so much?
A. Building-plan layouts for the plant were frozen at an early date to permit construction to start in the fall of 1962. As engineering developed, it was apparent that more space would be required. The least costly solution was to provide elevated space rather than to make drastic engineering changes in the total plant configuration.

Q. Why the sudden jump in forecast cost of several millions?
A. Previously, no allowance was made to cover start-up equipment modifications and rearrangements necessary to make the plant operational.

Q. The project's major scope was to relocate four existing plants. Why should there be any omissions or unknowns?
A. Individually, the processes were estimated in detail; however, in fitting all of these product lines into a single building complex, there was a lack of understanding for estimating the magnitude in providing space or services.

Q. Were the Dover omissions and unknowns with respect to processes and equipment greater than in other types of plants Bechtel has constructed?
A. Bechtel has stated that Dover is the most complicated plant it has ever designed or constructed.

Q. Where are the major items or differences in equipment cost now versus what was included in the original authorization?
A. The cost of some equipment installations increased substantially on completion of the engineering. For example, ten specific major items alone amount to nearly $2 million.

Q. What supplementary items have been included at Dover and appropriated separately since the project was begun?
A. A second spray tower plus ten other major items. Included above is a half million of unidentified contingency.

Q. Are you confident that the project can be completed within the supplement desired?
A. Yes.

Q. If another facility of this type were to be built in the future, what would you do differently to provide a more accurate cost estimate?
A. We would have to wait for completion of final engineering. We realize now that there were gaps in our knowledge, based on

> lack of past experience, for which we should have compensated with a request for a truly large contingency fund. However, a decision would have to be made as to whether the potential savings were attractive enough to offset the risk of proceeding with a possible overrun exposure. The Dover plant would have been delayed 12 months if we had waited for final engineering to be completed before starting construction—with a penalty of losing several millions in annual savings. In total, the project cost would not have changed appreciably. Experience gained from the Dover project would be used to review preliminary engineering estimates to minimize exposure to gross omissions of space, equipment, and building services.

Having thus provided the rationale for the need for further funds and having identified the justification for the request, the Jell-O/Dover staff set about the preparation of the formal presentation that the operations manager would then submit to the operating policy committee with the expectation that it would then be sent on to the board for discussion and approval.

In making its presentation for a large, supplemental capital fund appropriation, the staff examined every element that had entered into the original estimate of August 1962. Then followed the session of self-put questions and answers, during which every aspect of the earlier appropriation was reexamined and then modified or enlarged in the light of present needs and future likelihoods. It was in this framework that the staff hammered out a supplemental request that went to the operating policy committee and thence, on May 6, 1964, to the board. It was a forthright document—and in step with the dynamics of the industry. Its ready admission that earlier sights had been set too low, backed up with full particulars of the reasons why, made it a reassuring petition.

The main provisions of the supplemental request shaped up as follows:

> *Dover—General.* Justification for building the plant: the decision was and is sound even though cost is much greater than originally estimated. The savings which justified the decision are now firm, and additional savings opportunities are now identifiable. The Dover plant permits improvements in housekeeping, sanitation, and consistent product quality which could not be achieved in the plants being closed. These "nonfinancial" benefits assume greater importance because of the emphasis that GF, the Government (Food and Drug Administration), and customers are placing on this aspect of the food business. Moreover, the Dover plant is already giving GF an ability to expand that was not available in the old

plant locations. The second spray tower installation for Dream Whip and Whip 'n Chill is an example of the dynamics of Jell-O/ Dover.

Dover—Estimating Complexity. The Dover plant will provide facilities for the equivalent of seven different food industries (desserts, rice, chocolate, coconut, etc.) producing 50 different products and using many different raw materials. Each business involves many different processes—for example, cooking, spray drying, roasting, steam drying, wet mixing, dry mixing, and blending. The Task Force had no adequate background from which to estimate so complex an operation. There was insufficient experience in dealing with so many diverse functions in one place simultaneously. As a result, and with only 10 percent of the engineering complete at the time of the original estimate, the required number of changes, additions, and modifications of the original drawings was not foreseeable. It is now clear that a much larger contingency fund should have been requested.

Dover—Business Dynamics. Each of the seven basic branches of the food industry has been extremely active in aggressive marketing, product development, and cost reduction programs. Improvements and modifications in each product area have been identified as final engineering progressed. Examples: beefing up with structural steel in the Dream Whip area for a second tower; extending the sanitary floor in the rice area; providing space for a new type of bean-roasting equipment. There are 3,460 pieces of new equipment and 2,200 old ones to be installed. At the time of the original authorization many of the new pieces were still to be finalized in design with manufacturers, and performance specifications were yet to be agreed upon. In many instances, supporting equipment and controls had not been designed. Of the 2,200 pieces identified to be moved, some were found to be impractical to move after all.

Dover—Expediting Savings. The basic reasoning of the Task Force has been to achieve savings—several millions per year—as soon as possible. Many of the decisions made and actions taken over the past two or three years stemmed from a desire to expedite these savings. This is what caused construction to be started before engineering was completed. It is estimated that the project (and the savings) would have been delayed nine to twelve months if construction had been postponed until after the completion of engineering.

Dover Plant Status Report. To realize how rapidly the Dover plant is approaching reality, consider: Hoboken closed April 6, 1964. All coconut, Log Cabin, Jell-O Gelatin, and Jell-O Puddings previously produced there are now in production at Dover. Packing-line efficiencies are equal to or better than plan. LeRoy is scheduled to be shut down July 31, 1964; Orange will be kept open temporarily after transferring all of the rice and tapioca processes to Dover; Dorchester shutdown is set for September 28, 1964.

Dover Project Annual Savings. Categories here are: Number of Employees, Labor Rates, Supplies and Expenses, Materials Costs and Yields, Property Taxes and Utilities. The Task Force listed its current estimate of savings in each of these categories as compared to the figures submitted in August 1962. Overall, the current figure totals half a million dollars more than the original. Specific analysis is given as follows:

> Number of Employees: Substantial increase in dollar savings is due to a greater reduction of people than previously estimated (original manpower reduction estimate was 509 people; now it is 576). Manning tables have now been developed in detail for each department, and the Task Force is confident that annual savings of several millions can be realized.
>
> Labor Rates: Savings are based on current estimates for Dover versus current rates posted at the four plants. The August 1962 savings were based on estimated Dover rates versus then-current rates at the four plants.
>
> Supplies and Expenses: This includes maintenance materials and supplies, stationery, travel, telephone, outside warehousing, demurrage, publications, etc. The August 1962 estimate was based on reduced number of employees while the current estimate is much more accurate since it is based on detailed department budgets.
>
> Material Costs and Yields: Improved plant layout will provide at least $200,000 per year in savings, with potential for even more.
>
> Property Taxes and Utilities: Here there is a decline in savings, due to greater electrical power consumption than previously estimated (larger connected load) and slight increase in taxes because of the annexation of the plant area into the City of Dover.

Other Expenses. Three categories here: Dover One-Time Expenses, Loss on Present Plants, Employee Terminations and Transfers. The current estimate on One-Time Expenses is up a million from the August 1962 figure. The same holds true for the second category, Loss on Present Plants. The current estimate here involves idle plant expense for a one-year retention of Hoboken and a two-year retention of the other three plants after production shutdown. Lack of firm offers may make it necessary to request additional funds from the board. The estimate for Employee Termination & Transfers remains unchanged. Here is an area where the Task

Force has a wealth of experience to draw upon. Accordingly the estimate of both the number of people affected and the average cost per person will be very close to the August 1962 estimate.

Dover Project Costs. Categories here, for comparison with the earlier estimates, include: Land, Buildings, Equipment and Utilities, Engineering. Current estimate is up several millions, for which the following reasons are adduced: Land: No change. Buildings: Substantially increased cost is due to fact that the exterior plant layouts were frozen at an early date to permit construction to start in the fall of 1962. But as the engineering developed, it became apparent that more space would be required in the center areas of the complex for a special computer room system, motor control centers, electrical switch gears, and ingredient handling. Least costly solution was to provide elevated space rather than make drastic engineering changes in total plant configuration. Total square footage was upped from 817,000 to 1,023,000 because of the necessity to construct the mezzanines, platforms, and elevated slabs, which were not included in the earlier estimate. During final engineering, estimates were found deficient for adequate food-plant sanitation, safety, roof revisions and penetrations, hose stations, lighting, and additional interior walls and doorways. Equipment and Utilities: Also substantially increased for many of the same reasons already outlined. There was insufficient allowance made to cover start-up modifications and equipment rearrangements necessary to make the Dover plant operational. Also, major additional equipment items with significant cost impact were defined in final engineering in ten categories. Engineering: The greater complexity of the Dover plant caused a substantial increase in the engineering account. None of us was aware of the gaps in our engineering and estimating knowledge at the time. Actually, a major effort was made to relocate all processes as installed at the four existing plants, rather than engineer equipment-innovation or automation features. This was done not only to hold down equipment cost but also to minimize start-up risk. But it was only partially successful because the dynamics of the business (new products, new packs, new processes) forced more changes than originally anticipated. And, moreover, final engineering disclosed that it was not feasible to duplicate in Dover some of the equipment, layouts, and processes in the old plants. So while it is apparent that a very substantial capital supplement will be required to complete the project, this by no means detracts from the soundness of the basic decision to construct Jell-O/Dover. It is a fine facility, well engineered and well planned for efficient operation. There is tremendous enthusiasm on the part of all the people working directly on the project.

Such was the pattern of the presentation as well as the justification for the additional funds requested. There were, of course, charts and tables to illuminate the various sections, and the figures were precisely delineated.

Speed continued to be the basic motivating force that had activated the two years of arduous planning, projecting, procuring, moving, installing, and finally—re-estimating. Management from the top down was in agreement on one point: shoot for the maximum savings at the earliest possible moment.

The request for several millions in supplemental funds was promptly approved, and work at Jell-O/Dover moved ahead without the loss of a single day.

SHUTDOWN AND STARTUP

Chapter V

SHUTDOWN AND STARTUP

As the structure of the new plant began to take shape, attention was turned to the installation of processing and packaging equipment. There were approximately 5,600 major pieces of equipment to be installed in the new four-in-one plant; 3,400 pieces of new equipment; and 2,200 to be relocated from the four old plants. The shutdown of the old plants—production line by production line—and the startup of the new plant, with its blend of old and new equipment, required a carefully worked out plan which, at the same time, provided the flexibility to take into account delays in construction which might in turn delay equipment installation. Major delays, of course, would have serious effects on the Jell-O Division's inventory position with the risk of jeopardizing its product franchises by failure to supply customers. Also affected would be various marketing and sales promotion plans.

It was clear that the closest sort of teamwork was needed among the engineering, production, sales, and marketing people. The Jell-O

Division operations manager summed up the teamwork concept in a letter to all plant managers in October 1962:

> At our (September) operations meeting . . . we established areas of responsibility for operating and shutting down our present plants and for planning, constructing, and starting up the new facility. In general, each local manager was assigned the responsibility to operate and shut down the plant under his control, and the Facilities Improvement Group was assigned responsibility for the new plant planning, construction, and startup. In order to carry out this assignment, a number of key people have been or will be transferred to that group.
>
> We have discussed many times the absolute requirement that none of the Jell-O Division's product franchises be put in jeopardy by our failure to make finished products available to customers and consumers during the move and startup of the new plant. This means that we must take advantage of all available knowledge and experience in order to insure that the new plant be well planned, well constructed, and well staffed. It is also important that our premove inventory planning and postmove start-up scheduling be done in a way that minimizes risk.

The critical path method, which was employed in determining the plant construction schedule, was also used to set up a schedule for moving and starting up various administrative functions at the new plant. It proves to be a very valuable tool because it demanded the following:

1. Planning in depth before scheduling.
2. Effective utilization of manpower with recognizable results.
3. Evaluation of major changes in plans to provide a minimum disruption in manpower and maximum assurance of fulfillment according to schedule.
4. Coordination among all areas involved in the move.
5. Continual checking of construction schedule changes to evaluate the effect on administrative functions.

The critical path diagram for the administrative functions scheduled the move and startup of various accounting functions prior to all other activities. In fact, accounting was largely transferred to Dover before plant office facilities were completed. Office space was leased and the computer, which would eventually be in the plant, was installed in the temporary quarters. This allowed a longer shake-down period on transfer of many accounting and production planning operations to computer programs. Accounting functions were taken over from the four old plants as rapidly as possible. In some cases, long-distance data transmission was used to allow accounting operations for the old plants to be handled at Dover.

Later stages of the move, as determined by the critical path method, involved personnel activities; purchasing; and the planning, scheduling, operations, and inventory control of the various product lines. The required inventory buildups were calculated for each product line on the basis of a preferred moving schedule which, in turn, depended upon meeting the construction schedule at Dover. Calculations were also made for a three-month and six-month delay in executing the various moves. In figuring the buildups, production planners assumed that equipment would be removed and reinstalled on a two-shift, five-day-per-week operation, that a fixed number of days would be required to transport equipment from each plant to Dover, and that during the first eight weeks of operation in the new plant efficiencies would average one-half of normal.

The inventory buildups were accomplished at the old plants by adding extra shifts and with overtime work on weekends. Storage of the excess inventory of Jell-O's grocery product lines was handled by the company's regular distribution-sales services warehouses. However, some of the bulk product inventory was stored in leased warehouse space. Calculations were made of funds invested, penalty costs (extra shifts, overtime), and storage costs of all excess inventory. The planners estimated that a one-shift operation on installation of equipment at the new plant would increase inventory requirements and costs by 25 percent. Further increases could result from a shortage of trained personnel to install and start up the equipment, by sales which exceeded forecasts, by any equipment breakdown which required long repair time, or by loss or damage of equipment in transit.

While careful planning could minimize risk, it could not eliminate it. The dynamic character of the food business could—and did—cause situations which upset the best-conceived sales projections upon which the inventory buildups had been based. For example, in early 1963—with plant construction just getting well under way—consumer demand for Dream Whip, a spray-dried product, far exceeded sales estimates. It was soon obvious that spray-drying equipment and auxiliary machinery at the Dorchester plant could not build up enough inventory to cover the downtime required for moving certain pieces of the equipment to Dover. Signals had to be changed in a hurry. Instead of moving the Dorchester equipment, new machinery was ordered for installation at Dover while the equipment at the Dorchester plant was kept in operation.

Similar situations were destined to occur throughout the move, and the Dover plant staff was faced with a "chess game" type of planning in which the picture changed from day to day. Always under consideration was the interrelationship among building completion schedules, equipment installation, inventory, and sales with the protection of product franchises getting heavy emphasis.

Another complicating factor was the necessity to keep abreast of marketing plans for changed package designs, special promotions, and various "cents off" deal packs. New package designs sometimes made it necessary to alter equipment in the midst of the move or to plan for the installation of new equipment. Promotional or "deal" packs affected the staffing of both old and new plants as well as rates of production.

Moreover, the Jell-O Division was engaged in a business where the introduction of new products was a way of life that could not be abandoned during the plant consolidation. New products which were "on stream" at the time of the move had to be absorbed into the new plant as they came to fruition. This, of course, meant adding more production lines and new equipment and throwing an additional burden on warehouse and shipping facilities.

For example, in the midst of booming sales of Dream Whip, the division introduced a new product called Whip 'n Chill which was also spray dried. Demand for the new product made it necessary to install an additional spray-drying tower in the new plant, a development that had not been planned to take place for several years.

In some cases when the inventory of certain products fell below the desired level, plans called for other production facilities of the Jell-O Division—the Calumet plant in Chicago and facilities located in Maxwell House plants in San Leandro, California, and Houston, Texas—to increase production. In other cases when the Dover plant had production but not packaging capability, the bulk product was shipped to co-packers.

Several months before the first piece of equipment was moved from the old plants, the corporate engineering department produced a detailed procedure on the relocation of equipment. A covering memorandum read as follows:

> The move requires the cooperation of assigned people in the four existing plants and Dover, the Bechtel organization, the traffic

> department, a rigging and moving contractor, and corporate engineering.
>
> The overall coordination of these groups will be under the direction of a Relocation Manager of the Project, who will report directly to the Associate Director of Corporate Engineering.
>
> Scheduling of each move is of great importance to the Jell-O Division. Any deviation from the general project schedule should be brought to the immediate attention of the Relocation Manager.

The relocation procedure involved keeping a schedule—brought up to date as necessary—for each identified move of equipment. This schedule, kept by the Bechtel organization, showed the following steps:

1. Completion of Dover building ready for receiving relocated equipment.
2. Completion of utility services to the area.
3. Installation of new equipment necessary for production.
4. Modification of existing equipment.
5. Plant shutdown dates.
6. Disconnecting, tagging, and removal of platforms, ducts, and so on.
7. Cleaning and modifying equipment.
8. Making equipment available to rigging or moving contractor.
9. Shipping to Dover.
10. Unloading and rigging into place.
11. Connecting of utility services to equipment.
12. Testing for mechanical startup.
13. Startup and operation to full capacity.

The following are excerpts from the detailed descriptions of each step of a move:

> The Bechtel relocation representative will notify the Relocation Manager of completion dates of the building and when it is ready to receive relocated equipment.
>
> The building area which will house the move should be substantially complete, waterproof, and dust free.
>
> Corporate Engineering representatives on the job will review all drawings in their respective areas in advance of the scheduled move to see that all foundations, floor penetrations, and so on are in place.
>
> When large equipment is involved, Corporate Engineering per-

sonnel in the field will review with their counterparts in the Bechtel organization the methods to be used in getting the equipment into place. This will include the availability of elevators, truck unloading facilities, wall openings, and so on.

In many cases it is necessary to implement relocated production lines with new equipment. Delays in receipt of this equipment will obviously delay the startup of the facility.

Corporate Engineering area engineers, Bechtel, and General Foods Procurement will keep the Relocation Manager informed of all delays in delivery and installation of new equipment required to complete each relocated line.

Bechtel responsibility includes the startup of new equipment to the point where it is ready to receive product.

Certain existing equipment must be modified in order to fit into the reassembled process line. Wherever possible this equipment is modified by the four plants in advance of shutdown.

Plant personnel will prepare all relocated equipment for removal by the riggers and mover. This will include disconnecting all conduit and wire, piping, duct work, platforms, and so on which connect to the building.

Plant shutdown dates are shown for each major move on the Bechtel project schedule. Any modifications of these schedules as a result of inventory or production problems will be identified by the Dover Relocation Coordinator. The Relocation Manager will study with Bechtel the effects of these moves on the overall schedule. If no major problems arise, a revised schedule will be issued.

All equipment will be in good operating order prior to moving. Plant personnel will have equipment cleaned and modified before riggers arrive.

A plant representative will be designated to supervise when major equipment must be disassembled by the rigger. . . . This same representative will be made available to supervise reassembly at Dover.

Receiving, unloading, and rigging into place will follow the same procedures established by Bechtel for new equipment.

Corporate engineers shall witness all startups and recommend to Jell-O that the equipment is ready for takeover.

The first relocation of equipment was made in early November 1963 from the Walter Baker plant in Dorchester. It was planned as a pilot move to check out procedures in dismantling, rigging, shipping, unloading, and rigging into place in the new plant. Another pilot move—this time of large equipment from Hoboken—was made a few days later. As expected, neither move went smoothly; and the Relocation Coordinator arranged for the rigging contractor to hold ''rehearsals'' of all future moves in order to determine access routes, spotting of cranes, use of elevators, and so forth. This procedure eliminated considerable potential trouble and delay.

There were three alternatives in planning the movement of equipment: (1) build up sufficient inventory to cover the downtime necessary to move equipment to Dover, install it, and begin production; (2) get new equipment into production at Dover before shutting down lines at the old plants; and (3) where possible, move and start up a portion of the equipment while leaving other lines in production at the old plant.

In the cases of LeRoy, Orange, and Hoboken, one or the other of the first two methods was used. Much of the LeRoy plant's processing and packaging equipment was being replaced with new machinery at Dover. Thus new lines were in production before old equipment was moved. In addition, Jell-O desserts were also produced at the Calumet plant in Chicago and in the Maxwell House Division plant at San Leandro, California. Stepped up production at these plants could be used to keep inventories at a safe level. Rice and tapioca production lines at the new plant were a blend of old and new equipment. Therefore, the inventory buildup had to be sufficient to supply customer demand during the period between shutdown at Orange and startup at Dover. In addition, however, there was rice production capacity in the Maxwell House plant at Houston, Texas, which could assume part of the load. The same sort of situation prevailed in the Hoboken move, except that the Franklin Baker plant was the sole source of coconut.

By far the most difficult move was the Walter Baker chocolate plant. The move involved approximately 180 truckloads of equipment. Extremely complex equipment is required for chocolate production, and much of the equipment at Dorchester was scheduled for transfer to Dover. Some new equipment had been installed at Dorchester for shakedown and testing before being installed at Dover.

It was impossible to build up sufficient inventory to cover the time required to shut down, move, and start up the Walter Baker plant in one stage. Therefore, it was done in three phases, the first of which consisted almost entirely of new equipment. Other new equipment had been installed at Dover, giving the new plant the capability of roasting cocoa beans and producing the basic chocolate "liquor." The second phase of the move involved approximately 50 percent of the Dorchester plant's capacity to produce chocolate liquor, cocoa powders, and chocolate coatings, plus its total capacity for grocery items such as unsweetened baking chocolate and German's chocolate. In the third phase, Dorchester's remaining capacity for producing bulk chocolate was moved to Dover.

Constant adjustments in schedule were necessary throughout the entire shutdown-and-move period. Construction delays and missed schedules in delivery of new equipment to Dover sometimes resulted in changing the entire relocation timetable for one or more of the old plants. And, each time this occurred, there were changes in inventory plans, costs, personnel training dates, transfer dates, hiring dates, and so on. For example, the first phase of the Dorchester move fell approximately three months behind schedule, necessitating a speedup of the second phase in an attempt to regain some of the lost time. Such a speedup made it necessary for the building contractor and subcontractors to increase manpower on the job, add extra shifts, or work overtime. This, of course, added to the cost of construction.

The removal of equipment from the Hoboken plant was completed first, and the plant was closed in April 1964. The LeRoy plant completed its shutdown in July 1964, and the final phase-out of production at Dorchester came in December of that year. However, spray-drying operations at the Dorchester plant were kept running to supplement the production of the two new spray-drying towers at Dover. In March 1964, with the move of people and equipment from the Orange plant partially completed, the Jell-O Division decided to use the plant for an indefinite period to do experimental work on some new products. Approximately 35 employees were retained at Orange for this work.*

The first two production lines at Dover began operation in January 1964. One line—involving a high-speed packaging machine for Jell-O gelatin dessert—was new equipment. Another—a can- or bottle-filling line for syrup—had been moved from Hoboken. The high-speed Jell-O line was operating at Dover before a similar line was shut down at Hoboken and transferred to Dover.

*As of February 1966, the status of the four old plants was a follows: The Hoboken plant was sold in October 1964. The Walter Baker plant in Dorchester was sold in four parcels in December 1964 and in June, July, and November 1965. The Orange plant was still being used for experimental and test market production of new products. The LeRoy plant was given to the people of the community and was to be under the jurisdiction of the LeRoy Development Corporation.

Throughout the remainder of 1964, more and more lines were started at the new plant. It is difficult to pinpoint any particular date as being the time when the plant reached so-called full production. The prime contractor, Bechtel, completed all work on the basic project in October 1964, but other contractors and subcontractors remained on the job to perform modifications and to install additional equipment to handle new products or to further mechanize some of the existing lines. Some such work was still in progress in the spring of 1965.

The startup of production lines did not always go smoothly. It was inevitable that there would be some design and construction deficiencies in a new plant as large and complex as Jell-O/Dover. For example, in some production areas the dust-collection system proved to be inadequate, and a consulting firm was retained to correct the problems. In other areas there was insufficient air conditioning, and the capacity had to be increased. Start-up operations almost always revealed minor—but important—problems in electrical systems, drainage systems, piping, pumps, valves, and so forth, which had to be corrected before full-scale production could begin.

One major problem occurred in the startup of rice production. This was caused not by in-plant troubles but by a delay in completion of a secondary sewage-treatment plant being constructed for the city. Rice processing was scheduled to begin in the summer of 1964. However, with the additional sewage treatment capacity not available, the starchy effluent of the rice would have been released into a nearby river where it would have created an odor problem, particularly during warm weather. Therefore, production of rice was delayed until late fall, and GF's Houston, Texas, plant kept its production at a high level to assure adequate inventories.

It was not a matter of merely pushing a button and having the line begin to run. Almost every piece of major equipment—even that moved from the old plants—went through a period of de-bugging, adjustment, and modification. This work was sometimes hampered by a shortage of experienced packaging-machine mechanics and, in the early stages, by a lack of replacement parts since the plant stores department was not yet fully stocked. During some critical periods of the startup, engineers and maintenance craftsmen were "borrowed" from other GF plants, and considerable assistance was obtained from equipment suppliers. As might be expected, new high-speed packaging lines and automated materials handling systems provided some of the knottiest start-up problems since maintenance personnel—even those from the four old plants—had little or no experience with such equipment.

Another problem during the startup phase was the maintenance of the required level of plant sanitation. Even the initial cleaning of the plant and equipment was a formidable task which often necessitated the assignment of large crews of clean-up men to the various areas of the plant as they were completed and turned over to Jell-O for operation. Also, it was frequently necessary to begin operations in one part of an area before construction and equipment installation were completed in the entire section. In such cases it was sometimes necessary to isolate production areas with temporary barriers of plywood or plastic.

As had been expected, the training and indoctrination of new employees was a continuing task during the start-up phase. Training manuals and standard operating procedures were prepared for each department, and in some cases experienced personnel, both from the four old plants and other GF plants, were brought in to instruct the newly hired employees in the techniques of operating the equipment. It was necessary to "overman" some departments or critical production lines while employees were learning operating procedures.

Improved safety and plant sanitation, plus the possibility of better quality control, were high among the many opportunities afforded by the new plant. However, many of the new employees were totally inexperienced at working in an industrial plant. It was necessary to train them in the rules and regulations of safety, sanitation, and plant housekeeping as well as in the basic concepts of quality control. Lectures and films were helpful in the safety and sanitation areas, but quality control continued to be a problem until a visual presentation was developed. This consisted of a sound tape and slide program centering around the quality control problems peculiar to each product. Slides were made at the plant, using employees in the role of consumers and plant workers. Each presentation began by showing typical consumer complaints and demonstrating what could be wrong with the product that reached the consumer. Following slides showed how each defect could have been prevented by proper quality control procedures on the production lines. The programs were highly successful, not only in reducing the amount of rejected product but also in inducing employee suggestions for quality-oriented production improvements.

Warehousing and shipping also proved to be knotty problems during the plant start-up period. Warehouse space at the new plant—with the exception of storage for cocoa beans and coconut—was sufficient only for minimum quantities of raw materials and approximately two days' production of finished goods. Thus the flow of raw materials into the plant and the outgoing shipment of finished products had to be carefully managed and coordinated with the railroad and trucking firms. As in most new operations, time was required to achieve smoothness.

One major difficulty was encountered on inbound shipments of sugar. When in full operation, the new plant had storage capacity for just under a two-day supply. So a continuous flow of inbound sugar shipments was required. When this was interrupted, it was necessary to supplement rail shipments of sugar with more costly truck shipments.

During much of the plant start-up phase, warehousing was complicated by the need to store larger-than-normal stocks of products which did not meet specifications or quality standards but which could be reprocessed and reclaimed. Further storage problems were created by the transfer of raw materials, packaging materials, and finished goods from the four old plants as they were closed. Frequently, during this period, there was a three-shift, seven-day-per-week production of spray-dried products which built up an in-plant inventory faster than it could be packaged and shipped. All of these extraordinary demands for storage space made it necessary to lease warehouses in the vicinity of the plant and to incur extra costs for the transfer of materials.

Various problems of the plant start-up phase continued over a longer period of time than originally estimated. Efficiencies on some processing and packaging lines did not rise to normal on schedule, and mechanical problems with certain new equipment continued to appear long after the initial startup. This, of course, affected the inventory position of some products—a contingency not covered by the inventory buildups. There were times when inventories of some products dipped dangerously low, necessitating extra shifts at Dover and boosts in production at other Jell-O Division plants. In this way the Division was able to protect its grocery franchises. However, it did encounter some out-of-stock positions on bulk products.

Obviously, the shutdown and start-up period brought many unforeseen problems, delays, and frustrations, both at the four old plants and at Dover. Some problems were peculiar to the packaged-food business; others could occur in any plant move of this magnitude. Not even the most meticulous planning and scheduling, computer programs, critical path methods, and so on can predict all problems; but sound management can solve them as they appear.

PERSONNEL POLICIES

Chapter VI

PERSONNEL POLICIES

The Jell-O Division general manager set the tone of GF's policy toward the employees of the four affected plants when he said, "We hope that everyone who can transfer to the new plant will express a wish to do so." This open invitation to transfer was motivated by several considerations. In addition to management's desire for fair and equitable treatment of the 1,800 employees, many of whom had been with the company for 20 or more years, there was the practical consideration that experienced employees would be needed to start up and operate the new plant. The offer of jobs for all was also an important factor in maintaining employee morale at the four old plants which were to remain in operation until the new plant was capable of taking over production.

Throughout the entire consolidation management adhered strictly to GF's long-standing policy of keeping all employees fully informed. This policy had been put to the test in previous moves, where it had demonstrated its value in building employee goodwill while at the same time effectively combating the always present rumor mill.

Thus employees at the four old plants were the first to know of the March 7, 1962, decision by GF's board of directors. Letters, bulletins, and news releases had been prepared and cleared with management well in advance of the scheduled board meeting. Three hours after the board took action, every employee at the four affected plants had been given a personalized letter from the general manager of the Jell-O Division and a copy of a news release scheduled to go to the press the following day. The following is the text of the letter:

> After thorough study and consideration of all the factors involved, General Foods has decided to consolidate four of the Eastern plants of the Jell-O Division into one modern production facility which probably will be located within 250 miles of New York City. This will mean the eventual closing of our plant at Hoboken, as well as the Jell-O plant in LeRoy, the Walter Baker plant in Dorchester, and the Minute plant in Orange.
>
> The attached press release, which is to go to the newspapers for publication tomorrow, will explain the scope of the move and give you an idea of the general background. Here, however, I would like to talk more at length about family matters.
>
> At the outset, let me assure you that you will be kept fully informed of developments as they occur, particularly of any move that may affect your future, and to begin with we'll want to tell you where the plant will be built just as soon as we know ourselves.
>
> Since the first relocation is more than a year away, we have plenty of time to establish the policies which will guide the move and to discuss the effect of the move on you personally. As soon as the site of the new plant is selected, and the engineering is far enough along to plan operating procedures, we can begin to talk about what jobs will be open, what qualifications will be needed, and how personal costs of transfers will be met. We hope that everyone who can transfer to the new plant will then express a wish to do so.
>
> For those who do not transfer to the new plant when the time comes, we will, of course, arrange suitable termination allowances based on age and length of service. Assistance to find other employment also will be available if needed.
>
> I realize that you will have many questions. Let me assure you that you will have a good opportunity to discuss your individual problems and that every consideration will be given each individual case.
>
> Jell-O and General Foods reached the important decision to consolidate our Eastern plants into one new facility with high hopes on the one hand but with a great deal of regret on the other. We have long enjoyed friendly relations in your community and our roots go very deep. We are aware that the move will cause everyone a certain amount of inconvenience and will greatly inconvenience some.

> We will do all we can to minimize personal inconvenience, and we believe that advance planning, shared with you, will help the most. Careful, forehanded, and shared plans certainly held personal inconvenience to a minimum when the General Offices moved from New York to White Plains in 1954, and that was a major move, too, involving about as many people as will be involved in our move. We will follow the same pattern, and I would like to emphasize again these three points:
>
> First, no job should be affected for more than a year, or longer.
>
> Second, in good time you will have your opportunity to discuss your personal future with us and learn precisely how the move will affect you.
>
> Third, you will be fully informed of developments as they occur.

This carefully drafted letter contained several notable points:

1. It did not beat around the bush in getting to its main message—that is, the plant where the employee worked was to be closed.
2. It did not go into a lengthy explanation of the company's reasons for the proposed move. Instead, it referred the employee to an attached press release and turned immediately to "family matters," which at this point were certainly the employee's greatest concern.
3. It immediately assured the employee that he would be kept fully informed of all developments—"particularly of any move that may affect your future."
4. It assured the employee that there was no sense of urgency or haste. The first relocation was more than a year away, and there was "plenty of time" to establish policies and to *discuss* the effects of the move.
5. It emphasized these points by repeating them at the end of the letter.

The news release accompanying the letter was a detailed announcement of the company's plans and the reasons behind them. It said that GF was planning to build a new, multimillion-dollar plant at a location "within 250 miles of New York City" and that a 50-acre site was being sought.

The release also pointed out that the proposed consolidation "had been studied by management very closely . . . with attention centered on whether to continue to invest in the existing plants or to build a new facility permitting major cost reductions through combined operations."

The release concluded that "there is no question but that building a new facility is an excellent business move which will best enable General Foods to maintain competitive leadership and improve our service to customers and the American consumer."

Of course, one immediate result of this announcement was a flood of sales pitches from countless communities from within—and some not within—the designated area. The company's handling of these presentations is discussed in the following chapter.

Following the original announcement, there was little to tell the employees for a period of several weeks. GF's engineers and consultants were proceeding with the preliminary engineering for the new plant, and site selection was under way. These activities were beginning to involve more and more people in the four old plants. News stories about the planned shutdowns and consolidation and all sorts of speculations about prospective plant locations were appearing frequently. Obviously, the situation was ripe for a flood of rumors among the employees. To forestall this, Jell-O's general manager dispatched a second letter to employees on May 15, 1962, to let everyone know that the company was considering Dover as the plant site:

> In keeping with our practice of informing you promptly of developments concerning the new consolidated Jell-O plant, we are attaching a copy of a news story which is being given to the press for release tomorrow. While no firm decision has yet been made as to the location of the new plant, one of the leading sites under consideration is in the Dover area where General Foods has obtained an option on some land. GF representatives are meeting today with officials in Wilmington, Delaware.

The following news story was released from Wilmington, Delaware, the next morning:

> Representatives of General Foods Corporation consulted here today with State of Delaware, Kent County, and City of Dover officials concerning the possible location near Dover of a consolidated processing plant for the company's Jell-O Division.
>
> The food company has obtained an option to purchase 115 acres in Kent County, bordering on the City of Dover. The company has been conducting a comprehensive study of possible locations.
>
> The company emphasized, however, that several fundamental questions remain to be settled before a decision can be reached to build in this area and on the particular site. Today's meeting was arranged to begin discussions of the area's resources in relation to

General Foods' requirements, including zoning, utilities, and other services.

Again, there was an inevitable period when there was nothing newsworthy to pass along to the employees. However, to allay apprehensions and put rumors to rest, the Jell-O general manager issued a third letter in July 1962, which said little except that there was nothing definite to say, but that progress was being made. He concluded by saying, "We know you are anxious—just as we are—to have this question of our location settled, and we just want to assure you again that you will be informed promptly when a decision is made."

The general manager's fourth letter to employees was sent to announce the final selection of Dover as the site for the new plant. It, too, was prepared in advance and delivered on the same day that the board of directors made its decision. Again, the letter was accompanied by a news release which would be given to the press on the following day. The letter read as follows:

> General Foods has settled upon Dover, Delaware, as the location for the new consolidated plant. Our Board of Directors today approved the capital expenditure for its construction. Ground breaking is scheduled for some time in October.
>
> As you know, extensive economic and engineering studies, as well as many discussions about our needs with public officials and others, were necessary. Out of these came the decision that takes us to Dover. Dover is near ocean shipping on which we rely for many raw materials, and it is close to the center of the big Eastern market for quick and economical shipment of our products. These considerations, among others, are vital if we are to hold our own in the highly competitive grocery business.
>
> Equally important, we think that Dover offers attractive living conditions and pleasant surroundings. Incidentally, just last month voters approved an annexation proposal which about doubled the area of the City of Dover and raised its population from about 7,500 to 12,500.
>
> Public officials there have been most cooperative, friendly, and helpful. The entire city has demonstrated genuine warmth and enthusiasm about the possibility of our becoming one of their business citizens.
>
> Final engineering relating to building design and construction, equipment specifications, and plant layout can now go forward immediately. A list of jobs in the new plant, together with qualifications and anticipated wage and salary rates based on a Dover community

> survey will be developed, and we should be ready for a discussion with you before the end of the year.
>
> Shortly you will receive a portfolio containing information with respect to the move as well as material prepared by Dover and state agencies on housing, schools, churches, local government, recreational opportunities, and other community services in and around Dover.
>
> If you want to be considered for transfer to Dover—and we hope you do—you may now want to plan a trip there at company expense, as outlined in the policy concerning transfer which you received early in May.

The news story was datelined White Plains, New York, and stated that Dover had been selected and all affected employees had been notified. It went on to describe the new plant as being basically of one-story construction occupying about 20 acres of a 115-acre site and stated: "It represents the largest single capital investment in General Foods history. Preliminary construction work is expected to begin in October. The property will be developed and landscaped in keeping with modern industrial park concepts."

The company's attitude toward the employees who would be involved in this shutdown and startup was expressed in these words:

> General Foods will give every consideration to employees at the four plants in which operations will be discontinued 12 to 18 months from now. It is the company's intention to transfer to the new facility those who wish to go and who are qualified to fill the jobs which will be available. The company will pay termination allowances and offer assistance in finding new employment to those who cannot make the move.

Thus during a six-month period employees at the four old plants had received four letters from the general manager of the Jell-O Division. Three letters had been accompanied by copies of news releases which were not distributed to the press until the following day. This procedure, it was felt, gave the employees the feeling of being the first to know of any important developments. One letter broke the rule of thumb that one should not say anything unless there is something worthwhile to say. However, it was felt that this letter served the purpose of letting the employees know that there had not been any developments which were being kept from them.

In addition, the four letters contained pledges of (1) a job for every employee who wanted to transfer and for whom there was a job available; (2) termination allowances and assistance in finding employment for those who did not want to move; (3) expense-paid trips to Dover for employees and their families; and (4) a continuing flow of information with respect to the move.

With the stage now set for transfer, termination, or retirement of employees, the task of further communications was turned over to the division operations manager. With the assistance of the company's public relations department, this direct and continuing community program was accomplished through a series of "On The Move to Dover" bulletins printed on a special and distinctive letterhead. An example is shown in Exhibit 1. These were packaged in a sturdy portfolio with packets for information "About Dover" and "About the Move." Included in the "About Dover" pocket were maps and aerial photographs of the Dover area plus travel guides and informational literature furnished by the Greater Dover Chamber of Commerce and the Delaware State Development Department. The "About the Move" pocket contained the company's "Review of Guidelines on Transfer and Termination" plus the first "On The Move" bulletin. The portfolio was designed to be retained as a ready file for information as it was received.

The first bulletin, dated September 21, 1962, was four pages long with a two-page centerfold carrying a reproduction of an architect's rendering of the new plant. The back page informed employees on the purpose and status of the new plant, while the front cover set the stage for all the bulletins to follow. Fifteen bulletins were destined to be tucked into the portfolio between September 1962 and July 1964.

There were five bulletins in 1962. One announced that the reimbursement allowance for those requesting permission to visit Dover would be increased; another stated that the salary and hourly pay rate for Dover had been determined and that the information would be made available to every employee through the plant managers; another dealt with engineering, ground-breaking plans, and the company's association with the Bechtel Corporation. One of these bulletins announced some personnel promotions in these terms:

> We have been studying ways to proceed as rapidly as is feasible with the final engineering to ensure that the new Dover plant is well designed and that its startup takes place with a minimum of expense and risk to our product franchises. The magnitude of the new plant and the complexity of relocating so large a part of our present operations have convinced us that it's essential to utilize

JELL-O Division Bulletin

ON THE MOVE TO DOVER

September 21, 1962

To Jell-O Employees at Dorchester, Hoboken, Le Roy, and Orange:

I hope this portfolio, "On the Move ... To Jell-O--Dover," will be informative and useful. It contains:

* A pocket for material about Dover, furnished by the city, the local Chamber of Commerce, the State of Delaware and other agencies.

* A pocket for material about the Move, which you will receive from the Jell-O Division from time to time to keep you fully posted about our plans.

You doubtless will want to keep the portfolio as a handy filing place for all such material. In addition to this bulletin -- which I hope will begin to give you a picture of what the new plant will be like -- there are enclosed an aerial picture of Dover and a review of the transfer and termination guidelines originally issued last May.

As Mr. Giblin indicated to you in his March 7 announcement of the proposed consolidation, such a step brings with it both anticipation and regret -- anticipation of what we will be able to accomplish with splendid new facilities strategically located, genuine regret that some old and pleasant ties must be severed.

We are deeply mindful that this move will create problems for many people. Our continuing desire and aim is to minimize personal inconvenience insofar as possible, through advance planning and through thoughtful consideration of each individual's particular situation.

You will find your supervisor and members of your personnel department ready and eager to help you in any way that they can in getting additional information you may want. But, quite frankly, there are many questions to which we don't yet have the answers. As we go along, however, we shall continue to advise you promptly -- through these "On the Move" bulletins and other material -- about all developments concerning you and the Dover move.

Thank you for your patience and understanding during this period which we appreciate is difficult for everyone.

Robert A. Stenninger

Division Operations Manager

EXHIBIT 1

> fully the operating know-how and experience in the Jell-O Division. At the same time it is necessary that we continue to operate our present plants as efficiently as possible.

This bulletin underscored one of the major dilemmas of the move and the startup of the new plant. While the best talent of the Jell-O Division (and perhaps of the entire corporation) was urgently needed at the new plant, it was necessary to retain skilled management and supervisory personnel at the four old plants. Thus, while key people were transferred to the new plant as rapidly as possible, some who were scheduled to occupy important positions at Dover were unavoidably involved at the old plants until they were shut down.

In 1963 there were eight "On the Move" bulletins. Three dealt with various aspects of shutdown and startup. One had to do with the seniority policy and rules for hourly employees. A second one announced the appointment of a local manager of community relations at Dover, a man who had grown up in the area and had much local press experience and acquaintanceship. Three bulletins dealt with matters of housing and the visits of employees and their families who wanted to take advantage of the company's invitation to come and look over the community where the new plant was being built and where a big GF family would reside.

As early as February 1963 more than 100 employees from the four plants had visited Dover, plus another 100 or so friends and relatives. In view of this, the Jell-O Division added an experienced local real estate consultant to the Dover staff to give all interested employees guidance and help on rentals and purchases of homes in Dover and other residential areas within a radius of 20 miles and to provide detailed counseling on mortgage matters.

By July 1963 almost 500 employees, plus their families and friends, had visited Dover. About 100 people had by this time rented apartments or bought homes in the area. Three new subdivisions were being developed. And as fast as new structures sprang up, listings on available living quarters were forwarded to the four plant managers. In less than three months, the visitor mark had passed 800, and 172 families had actually moved into Dover.

The 1963 "On the Move" bulletins were full of plant construction information. For instance, as of January all earth moving, grading, and drainage had been completed and much of the structural steel ordered. By July three-fourths of the structural steel was in place, and by September the final phases of the Dover consolidation had started. Production lines were being removed one by one from the old plants and being installed and started up at Dover.

While most of the 1963 bulletins dealt with information about the move, progress at the new plant, and plans for the future, the final bulletin of the year contained the following paragraph:

> We're mindful that for a wide variety of reasons many of you will find it impossible to go along with us to Dover. We want to assure you that the problems and concerns of those who aren't moving, as well as those who—fortunately for us—can go, will continue to be front and center in our thinking. Our personnel managers have been meeting with representatives of the appropriate state departments of labor, exploring the prospects for employment locally and the opportunities for people, if they wish to retrain, for new types of jobs.

In 1964 there were only two "On the Move" bulletins, one dated March 4 and the other July 2. Both dealt in depth with the status of the new plant. The final bulletin started out by saying, "As we come down the home stretch in the transfer of product lines and jobs in the old plants to Jell-O/Dover, we once more want to let you know how matters stand at each of the locations and how the schedule looks from here on out."

The Franklin Baker move had been completed on schedule in early April and the property had been sold. Transfer of tapioca and rice lines from Orange to Dover had been completed according to plan. Thirty-five employees elected to go to Dover. At Jell-O/LeRoy, there had been a series of scheduled production line shutdowns and transfers to Dover during the previous month. Final shutdown was to be July 31. A buyer for the plant was being sought, and LeRoy's civic leaders were lending splendid cooperation. At Walter Baker, all grocery chocolate lines had been shut down. Limited processing of several products was under way at Dover. Industrial chocolate lines were to be phased out in Dorchester by early fall.

This last bulletin closed with a typically informal rundown of the employee situation, in part as follows:

> Employee count at Jell-O/Dover has reached 930—365 of whom have transferred from the four old plants and 555 of whom were hired in Dover. 430 transferring employees have made housing commitments to date, and we are delighted to say that it appears likely that as many as 500 will make the move.

For well over two years now, we've been passing along information to you through these bulletins. We hope that they have served their intended purpose of helping you and your family well in advance to make plans which would serve your best interests.

Finally, we want to thank each of you for your loyalty, your understanding, and your good work from the beginning of the big move to the end of the upcoming final chapter.

A close study of the language and content of these bulletins is rewarding. Taken collectively, they show how one company communicates with its employees. The personality of the corporation is reflected in the text, and the policy of the organization is illustrated throughout.

During the entire span of time involved in the "On the Move" bulletin campaign, few news releases were issued as such. Yet there was a great deal of press coverage at all five communities, much of which came from the bulletins. They were interpreted by each paper in its own terms. Thus there was no aura of "boiler plate" about the stories; yet each was authentic and newsworthy.

Finally, the proof of the pudding being in the eating, it must be reported that 555 employees decided to transfer as a result, in part at least, of this program; 423 moved to Dover, 83 transferred to other plants of General Foods, and 49 moved to Dover from GF headquarters and other plants.

The Transfer, Termination, and Retirement Program

During this extensive flow of information on Dover developments, the personnel people were busy: first with the drafting of suitable policies on transfer and termination, and later on the manning tables for Dover. Precedents from earlier company moves were carefully studied and largely utilized.

For instance, as far back as 1946 criteria had been developed in connection with the shutdown of GF's Fairport plant in upstate New York. At that time concern for helping employees find other work was expressed in the following ways:

- Opening a job-placement bureau to canvass the community for jobs, to study each individual's job problem, and to advise him as to the best solution for his problem.
- Announcing the shutdown far enough in advance so that employees would have ample opportunity to look around.

- Trying to sell the plant to a new employer.
- Giving termination pay.
- Offering to shift employees to other plants.

By 1950 GF had outgrown its Maxwell House Coffee plant in Los Angeles and had built a new facility at San Leandro in the San Francisco area. All employees were extended the opportunity to make the move. Transfer policies included the following:

- Assurance that employees would have the same or an equivalent job in the new plant.
- Company-paid transportation for the employee, his immediate family, and his household effects.
- An extra living-cost allowance for as long as two weeks after departure from Los Angeles.
- Termination allowance based on age and length of service for those electing not to make the move. (In some instances this allowance amounted to as much as 25 weeks' pay.)
- A special closing bonus of 25 percent of the employee's last eight weeks' pay if he stayed until his job ended.
- Guidance in finding new employment.

In another instance, General Foods had moved its main offices from midtown Manhattan to suburban White Plains, New York, in 1954. Although this move was not comparable in every respect to moving a plant, it did provide the company with further experience in transferring people. Approximately 1,200 employees were involved in the Manhattan to White Plains move. As it had in previous cases, the company announced its plans to the affected employees well in advance, kept them fully informed of developments, and paid the expenses of employees who moved to the new location.

It was against the background of these established practices that the Jell-O Division's manager of personnel administration began an information program for all employees involved in the proposed consolidation. By May 2, 1962, a policy on transfer and termination was in circulation at all four plants. It was clear and concise:

> In recognition of the interest and concern of all employees in the benefits available to those who will transfer to the new plant and to those who will terminate their General Foods employment when the move to the new plant is made, the following policies have been prepared.
>
> I. It is General Foods intention to transfer to the new plant those employees who wish to go and who qualify for job openings on the basis of merit, competence, and length of service.

II. For those who do not transfer, it is General Foods intention to provide assistance in locating other suitable employment in the local area where they live. Termination allowance will be paid to those employees who qualify.

A more general policy statement was provided for all affected employees at the same time. It, too, had its roots in tradition. First, it assured everyone that information would be given the employees as soon and as often as the facts warranted. Then it promised that a "relocation desk" would be established in each of the four plants, whereby every employee would be posted on the move and provided with up-to-the-minute information on the status of his benefits as a help in deciding whether to move or terminate.

The employees were also told that a list of available jobs at the new facility was in the making along with a survey of prevailing salary and wage rates in the new plant community. All employees were informed that wages and salaries at the new plant would be based upon GF's stated policy of paying rates as good as those prevailing for similar work under similar conditions in the community where the plant is located.

As for helping those not transferring to locate jobs elsewhere, the following program was announced:

- Investigation of transfer opportunities to other nearby General Foods units.
- Investigation of employment opportunities with other employers in the area.
- Cooperation with the state employment services.
- Provision of various other kinds of assistance in each plant location.

The next step was to provide all the affected people with a detailed statement on reimbursement of moving expenses. A policy on termination was also distributed, along with full facts on company assistance available to those planning to dispose of leased or owned residences.

The extensive past experience of the company in dealing with plant moves helped the Jell-O Division to adapt to the situation. The established policies had proved fair and effective in the past; there was no reason to believe they would be any less effective and acceptable now.

As the manpower planning schedule for the new plant developed, a special statement on the company's seniority policy for hourly employees was prepared for all the workers at the four plants. This document was distributed January 11, 1963, with a bulletin from the local plant manager stating:

> As one of those who may be considering transfer, you are entitled to have a clear understanding of the regulations governing selection, promotion, layoff, and recall. That is why this document has been prepared and is being issued at this time.
>
> This seniority policy has been developed with due consideration for policies currently in effect at our four plants and anticipated operating requirements at our new plant. Protection of present employees has been a principal consideration in deciding upon these rules. The spirit of this policy is not expected to change, but specific parts may be changed as the need dictates.

This policy, like the others, was based on precedent. GF recognized the importance, both to employees and to the company, of long and continuous service. Of course, the company was also well aware of the necessity for having capable and qualified people in key jobs at the new plant. Thus in selecting employees for promotions, when fitness and ability were regarded as equal, length of service was the major deciding factor. And if a reduction in work force were to become a necessity, the same procedure would hold true in determining which employees to retain.

The policy statement first defined seniority and its application. Then it listed the four departments in the new plant: *Jell-O,* where most of the lines currently being manufactured in LeRoy, Orange, and Hoboken would be produced; *Chocolate,* where the Walter Baker chocolate products currently coming from Dorchester would be produced; *Maintenance and Utilities;* and *Receiving and Shipping.* The significance of the breakdown into departments lay in the fact that employees would exercise plant seniority within these departments for job advancement, layoff, and so forth. Another general provision of the seniority policy was that it applied separately to men and women.

As early as November 1962 a survey had been conducted among Dover's principal plants in order to determine the prevailing hourly wage rates and salaries. This survey was the determining factor in setting pay ranges for jobs at the new plant. These pay ranges were then furnished to the four plant managers, who were charged with the responsibility of transmitting the information to all concerned. The plant managers were to make sure that everybody understood the company's policy about paying salaries and wages as good as those prevailing for similar work under similar conditions in the communities where its plants and offices are located. At the same time, they were authorized to say that these rates would be adjusted if community pay levels in Dover should change at any time in the future. Moreover, it was made clear to the hourly workers that those who decided to request transfer to Dover and who qualified for higher-rated jobs would be given the opportunity to train for these better jobs.

Once the location of the new plant had been determined and the wage scales thus firmed up, the Jell-O Division operations manager set about making information available to the individual employees as to specific opportunities in Dover. The "relocation desk" technique was the means for doing this. By this method, people were identified in terms of existing jobs and positions and the company was able to learn a great deal about each individual in terms of his aspirations and aptitudes. This was a two-way street: it helped the Jell-O Division zero in on specific qualifications; it also gave each individual the opportunity to review his personal experiences and qualifications for possible job assignment elsewhere with the company or outside if the Dover move was out of his reach.

For salaried employees, an "individual qualification" form was provided for this purpose. (See Exhibit 2.) This form asked the individual to prepare an analysis of his unique qualifications. It provided an opportunity for each person to set down in his own way information on particular experience, accomplishments, education, skills, and job interests.

Once this form had been filled out, each individual knew that he would have an opportunity to discuss it with his supervisor. He understood, too, that the form would become the Jell-O Division's basic source file and that it was vital to his own best interests that the information be as complete, accurate, frank, and meaningful as possible. So important was this form regarded by headquarters that a special "guide sheet" was prepared for the persons conducting the interviews. (See Exhibit 3.) It indicated what the interviewer was to *listen* for and to *search* out, all to the end that the individual's qualifications, his business history, would be presented in the best possible light.

In July 1963 relocation desks were set up at the four plants. As of that date, GF's headquarters people had prepared "estimate of benefit" forms on all employees at each of the four plants and had sent these confidential studies on to the local managers to be turned over to the relocation desk representatives. With the information contained on the forms, plus the accumulated knowledge already assembled on each worker, it was at last possible to conduct personal interviews based on the fullest possible facts.

(text continued on page 110)

MANPOWER PLANNING—DOVER PLANT—PHASE I

For use by the INDIVIDUAL in preparing his individual qualifications

INDIVIDUAL QUALIFICATIONS OF: ______________________

Current Position: ______________ Birth Date ______________

Purpose: This is an opportunity to prepare an analysis of your own *unique* and *individual* qualifications. It is much like writing a resume but should not be regarded as a writing exercise. After you have included what you feel is important under each category, review and discuss it with your manager. Out of your discussion will come a summary of your talents and interests which should enable you and your manager to indicate the best use of your abilities for assignment at the Dover Plant.

The five categories are:

1) Work Experience and Knowledge
2) Major Accomplishments
3) Education
4) Job Interests or Preferences
5) Skills or Personal Abilities

I. *Work Experience and Knowledge* (What have I done?)
Working from past to present position, indicate:

- Type of work, function, level of responsibility with concise statement of purpose of position (if outside GF). Indicate size and kind of company and geographic locations.
- Specific job titles and service for positions within GF, explaining purpose of position.
- Include military experience and type, if any.
- A summary of what I've gained or learned from my experience—that is, the extent of knowledge, familiarity, understanding of functions, techniques, operations, i.e.
- Thorough knowledge of functional responsibility gained at plant, Division, and Corporate level.
- Thorough understanding of industry practices.
- Working knowledge of legal requirements and company policies relating to my specific activity.

EXHIBIT 2

II. *Major Accomplishments*

List, not in order of importance, any specific accomplishment or evidence of my ability from all of the work experiences above. What can I point to in a qualitative or quantitative way that shows initiative, leadership, or abilities to solve complex problems, etc., such as:

- Have increased sales volume over a certain period to a certain degree.
- Have reduced costs or have increased profits.
- Have had success in developing new ideas of some specific type.
- Have performed well under certain kinds of conditions such as pressures, budgets, deadlines, etc.

(*Note:* Initiated, managed, installed, adapted, assisted, changed, compiled, effected, executed, led, achieved, designed, created, awarded, commended, exceeded, negotiated, operated, purchased, processed, prepared, revised, selected, supervised, trained, administered, etc., are some words which may suggest accomplishment.)

III. *Education*

Level of education and if college, name of college or university and major. Special courses since graduation. Any special languages, licenses, or trades.

IV *Job Interests/Preferences*

What gives me satisfaction from a job? What things do I prefer? Line or staff? Working as an individual or as part of a group? Speaking? Writing? Long-range projects rather than immediate tangible results? Developing a new function or a "going" operation? Current versus long-range interests? Following a pattern versus being creative? Designing? Developing? Research? Administration?

V. *Skills/Personal Abilities*

What are my most effective skills and abilities? What do I do better than most people? Am I a stimulator of new ideas or am I a follow-through and "do" man? Do I make good verbal or written presentations? Am I able to gain cooperation without authority? Do I have a good numbers facility? Do I work well under pressure? Am I particularly good at talking customer, plant, or other's language?

EXHIBIT 2 (concluded)

MANPOWER PLANNING—DOVER PLANT—PHASE I

Guide sheet for MANAGER'S discussion with the individual on INDIVIDUAL QUALIFICATIONS

Purpose: A review of INDIVIDUAL QUALIFICATIONS is to remind you and each key person reporting to you of his qualifications so best use can be made of his particular experience, interests, and abilities. To prepare yourself for the individual's discussion with you, think about what you now know about him through your work contacts, discussions, any reference check made on previous jobs, his personnel record, salary information, comments of others, etc. Ask questions. He can rewrite his qualifications for further discussion if necessary.

The five categories of information he will cover are:

1) Work Experience and Knowledge
2) Major Accomplishments
3) Education
4) Job Interests/Preferences
5) Skills/Personal Abilities

I. *Work Experience and Knowledge*

Listen for *depth* and *kind* of experience by function (production, purchasing, marketing) level (managerial, non-managerial) type and size of company, geographical location. *Listen* for *knowledge* gained through these experiences, whether wide, limited, some or no knowledge of:

Company policies and procedures
Markets
Customers
Manufacturing processes
His area of specialty and closely related ones
Suppliers
Etc.

Get him to identify and summarize what he did and what he learned from each job inside or outside of GF.

II. *Major Accomplishments*

This is an important question that many people never considered. Search for *specific* accomplishment. Under what circumstances did he accomplish? Order

EXHIBIT 3

of importance is not significant. Think about what *he's done* as evidenced from reports, records, complaints, praise, commendations, awards, etc., and ***listen for specific results,*** rather than "what he did", such as:

Exceeded sales budget by . . .
Reduced operating costs by . . .
Added new accounts, namely . . .

Developed a new process, i.e. . . .
Improved safety record by . . .
Designed product machinery such as . . .
Reduced payroll by . . .

Words suggesting this are: initiated, managed, installed, adapted, assisted, changed, compiled, effected, executed, led, achieved, designed, created, awarded, commended, exceeded, negotiated, operated, purchased, processed, prepared, revised, selected, supervised, trained, administered, etc.

(*Note:* This is important to you when you look at his fiscal objectives. Are they going to make him *achieve* something more, or different from his past experience—or how much is he repeating? His objectives should be making him "stretch" beyond previous accomplishments.)

III. *Education*
Level and degree attained; special outside courses.

IV. *Job Interests/Preferences*
Listen for what seems to give him job satisfaction—for what his long-range goals might be. Do his interests match his abilities?

V. *Skills/Personal Abilities*
Think about how you've seen him work. Look for those skills and abilities for which he is known and is particularly strong:

Recognizing opportunities for change
Stimulating ideas and innovating
Utilizing services and sources
Analyzing and solving problems
Getting things done (a doer)
Making presentations and/or writing
Planning (short- or long-range)
Mechanical abilities
Scheduling
Training or motivating
Keeping useful records
Trouble shooting
Community activities
Negotiations with customers, suppliers, unions, and so forth

EXHIBIT 3 (concluded)

The "estimate of benefit" form was a four-page document whose purpose was to provide each individual with full knowledge of his status with the company, his rights, perquisites, and so forth, on the basis of which he could the more readily make up his mind about moving to Dover.

The centerfold of this form contained specific data concerning each employee. The personnel representative handling the relocation desk referred to these figures when he sat down privately with each individual and discussed his status with him. The form in Exhibit 4 covers a skilled worker who was 57 years old, at the time of the interview, and who had 25 years of continuous company service—in every sense a senior employee. Without question, this man had skills that were very much in demand at Dover, but at his age and with his family roots deeply embedded in his community, the chances were that he would prefer to accept termination and ask GF's help in finding local employment rather than make the move.

As a demonstration of the company's continuing interest in the individual who couldn't make the move, the Jell-O Division operations manager wrote this personal letter to every employee who decided to terminate:

> Now that the move to Dover has been completed, I want to express one last word of thanks for your service to General Foods and for your help in getting the final big job done.
>
> As we've said before, the decision was a difficult one to make on many scores, not the least of which were the personal problems it would cause the individuals concerned. Pulling up roots and leaving the plants where we've enjoyed such happy community relationships over the years, is a wrenching experience, believe me.
>
> We're very pleased that so many of the folks who were with the Jell-O Division in March of 1962 when the decision to move was announced were able to go along with us to Dover. We're genuinely sorry you couldn't go too.
>
> In the years to come we hope you'll have a warm feeling toward Jell-O and General Foods, just as we have for you as a result of our association and the job you helped us to accomplish.
>
> Best wishes and good luck to you in whatever you do.

The company's interest in each employee plus the potential for the future resulted in a substantial percentage of transfers. The figures in

(text continued on page 115)

The moving date of your plant is not yet known. However, we have prepared the following estimates of what your benefits will be as of July 1, 1963. All of the information shown for the Retirement and Life Insurance Plans is based upon GF's and your contributions as of the date of preparation of this statement plus an estimate of the additional benefits if you continue to contribute until July 1, 1963. Naturally, any change in your contributions to the Retirement and Life Insurance Plans will have an effect on the amounts shown for these plans. All benefits and privileges under the Retirement, Life Insurance, Accidental Death & Dismemberment, Medical Benefits, Termination Allowance, Vacation and Savings-Investment Plans are governed by the terms of these plans.

RETIREMENT

By continuing to contribute under the GF Retirement Plan on the basis of your earnings class as of September 1, 1961, your contributions will, as of July 1, 1963, amount to

① **$2,695.50**

Adding interest you will have

② **$3,283.50**

This money will be refunded to you

OR

If you leave GF and on July 1, 1963 will have *10 or more years of continuous service or prior to July 1, 1963 will have reached age 55* you may elect to leave your contributions and interest in the Plan and receive a yearly retirement income of

③ **$1,271.91**

beginning on....................

or if you elect to wait until age 65 before receiving any payments, your yearly retirement income will be

④ **$1,390.95**

If, prior to July 1, 1963, you will have reached age 55 and have 15 or more years of service and the income shown in box 3 is an increased amount determined under the special early retirement formula, this higher amount will be reduced beginning at age 65 to

⑤ **$ 941.67**

EXHIBIT 4

RETIREMENT *(continued)*

Other Retirement Plan features to be considered

Contingent Annuitant Option Level Income Option Widow's Benefit

In addition, for both men and women, Social Security Benefits may be payable in reduced amounts beginning at age 62.

LIFE INSURANCE

TERM INSURANCE (employees under age 45)

All term insurance will cease at the end of the month in which you leave GF, but if you die within the following 31 days, the full amount will be paid. During this 31 day period you may convert all or part of your term insurance without medical examination to an individual policy issued at the Aetna Life Insurance Company's regular rates. See attached statement for additional information on conversion.

Prepared for ____________________

Location ____________________

Please let us know Social Security # ____________________

if either of these ⟶ Date of Birth ____________________

is incorrect ⟶ Date Employed ____________________

PAID-UP INSURANCE (employees age 45 and over)

By continuing to contribute to the paid-up portion of the GF Life Insurance Plan on the basis of your earnings class as of January 1, 1962 your contributions will, on July 1, 1963, have purchased paid-up insurance which you may continue in force for life in the amount of

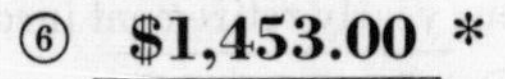

⑥ **$1,453.00 ***

Also, if you will have 15 or more years of service and have reached age of 55 on July 1, 1963, any non-contributory "gift" insurance which you may have will be continued in the amount of

⑦ **$ 500.00 ****

EXHIBIT 4 (continued)

LIFE INSURANCE *(continued)*

OR

If you elect to cancel your life insurance for its cash value on July 1, 1963 you will receive

⑧ $ 899.00

* If you will have reached age 55 with 15 or more years of service at separation date and you do not have any "gift" insurance (box 7), this amount, if less than $1,000 will be increased to $1,000 providing you have contributed continuously to the paid-up portion of the Plan since first eligible and provided you do not take the cash value shown in box 8.

** This amount, if less than $1,000, will be increased to $1,000 if you have contributed continuously to the paid-up portion of the Plan since first eligible to participate or have continued to purchase term insurance under the old Plan.

See attached statement for additional information on conversion.

An additional Life Insurance benefit to be considered—Widow's Benefit.

TERMINATION ALLOWANCE

If you continue working to within three months of your plant's moving date, you may be eligible for a termination allowance estimate (before tax) to be

⑨ $3,234.00

TOTAL PAYMENT FROM THREE SOURCES

If you are separated from GF and elect a refund of your contributions plus interest under the Retirement Plan, cancel your paid-up Life Insurance and also receive a termination allowance, your total payment, before tax, is estimated to be

⑩ $7,416.50

EXHIBIT 4 (continued)

MEDICAL BENEFITS

If you are a participant and you will have reached age 55 with 15 or more years of service at separation date, you may continue coverage for yourself and your dependents under the Basic part of the Plan at your present contribution rate. Basic benefits will be the same except that "hospital miscellaneous" charges will be limited to $500 during any one continuous period of disability. Major Medical benefits are not available.

If you do not meet the above eligibility requirements your coverage will be terminated at the end of the month in which you leave GF, but you will nevertheless have the opportunity to convert to an individual Aetna Life Insurance policy. See attached statement for additional information on conversion.

Maternity benefits will remain in force under the GF Plan to cover pregnancies existing on the date of termination of GF group coverage. Also, an extended benefit provision applies to employees or dependents who are wholly disabled on the date GF group coverage terminates.

EMPLOYEE SAVINGS-INVESTMENT

If you are a participant in this Plan, as soon as possible following termination or retirement the entire credit balance in your account will be returned to you—or within 30 days you may elect to use part or all of these funds to purchase shares of stock. If you resign or are discharged for cause your entire credit balance will be returned to you and you do not have the privilege of buying stock.

VACATION

You will receive pay in lieu of any unused vacation due you at time of separation.

UNEMPLOYMENT INSURANCE

Employees leaving the company because of the move may be eligible to receive Unemployment Insurance while they are seeking new employment, provided they meet the other qualifying provisions of state law. GF representatives will be acquainting the local Unemployment Insurance offices with facts about the plant move.

EXHIBIT 4 (concluded)

Exhibit 5, compiled in November 1964, tell the story in terms of each of the four affected plants. (The figures in the exhibit do not include employees who were still serving temporarily at the Orange and Dorchester plants.)

This, then, is a case history of one company's method of dealing on a person-to-person basis with the transfer, dislocation, and retirement of some 1,800 employees brought about by closing down four plants and consolidating them in a new facility. Whether the techniques and policies that governed GF's handling of the matter are of general application is difficult to say. What can be stated with conviction, however, is that it has worked well for this particular organization on numerous occasions in the past and seems to have done so in this latest and greatest of all the company's shutdown and start-up experiences.

This business of "open covenants openly arrived at," of reporting the bad as well as the good, is frankly considered by the company as an expression of self-interest. After all, each employee was a potential life consumer of company products, and in most cases there were whole families involved. But the fact remains that the tone of the bulletins and the scope of the termination and transfer allowances, and all other efforts support the promise made by the Jell-O Division's operations manager when he reported to management: "Figures cannot convey to you the very deep concern we feel for the 1,800 employees in our four Eastern plants. . . . It is our determination to be fair, considerate, and sympathetic with each employee in the best GF tradition."

It should be borne in mind that the above statement was *not* made to win employee confidence or loyalty or cooperation. It was made to management and has never been reported out prior to this. This makes all the more interesting a case history such as this one, since it shows *how* the operations manager went about doing with employees what he had committed himself to at the top management level.

PERSONNEL AND THE MOVE TO DOVER

	LeRoy	*Orange*	*Dorchester*	*Hoboken*
Number of employees as of March 1962	350	96	825	511
Transferred to Dover		34	187	114
Transferred to other GF units	11	3	11	58
Terminated with termination allowance	211	11	293	271
Retired, deceased, resigned	40	21	455	68

EXHIBIT 5

The Hiring Program

While some of Jell-O's personnel people were dealing with the problems of transfer, termination, and retirement of employees in the old plants, others were engaged in the largest and most concentrated hiring program in the company's history. During the calendar year 1964 nearly 1,400 new employees were hired at the new plant. (This was a greater number than the original estimates since new products had been introduced and the number of processing and packaging lines had been increased.)

The Jell-O Division opened an office in Dover in October 1962 and began issuing and accepting employment applications in May 1963. By September of that year more than 2,200 applications had been received for hourly employment and 914 for office work, and it was apparent that there would be a selection problem created by the sheer number of the applicants. A study of the applications also indicated that a substantial percentage of the candidates were obviously unsuited because of lack of experience, insufficient education, or even illiteracy. Some sort of objective testing was needed to reduce the number of applicants to manageable proportions.

The plant personnel department first considered administering its own tests. However, this had several obvious disadvantages: it would be expensive, it would require gross overstaffing of the department, and it might or might not produce valid results. Therefore, the personnel department asked for assistance from the Delaware State Employment Service, which offered to administer—free of charge—the General Aptitude Test Battery, a series of mental and manual aptitude tests designed by the U.S. Department of Labor and used on a nationwide basis by all state employment services for vocational counseling.

The complete selection process consisted of the General Aptitude Test Battery, an interview by a representative of the personnel department, another interview by a functional supervisor (foreman), a reference check, and a physical examination (including a back X-ray for men only). Each step was critical in that the applicant had to pass one step successfully before he could proceed to the next one. But only the functional interviewer could make a positive hiring decision, and all of the other steps were essentially "veto" processes. However, by July 1964 the combined pressures of employment interviewing and floor supervision became so great on the foremen that the functional interview was eliminated and positive selection authority was given to the personnel interviewer.

Through December 1964 the new plant had received 10,190 applications for hourly jobs. Of these, 9,220 were asked to take the battery of tests; 4,886 appeared for testing; 3,550 were interviewed; 1,456 were tentatively accepted; 1,284 passed the physical examination; 1,236 passed the reference check; and 1,113 were hired.

The General Aptitude Test Battery consists of eight subtests each designed to measure a specific skill or aptitude, three of which form the basis for what is generally called an I.Q. score. The norm for each subtest for all levels of literate employed people is 100.

The main virtues of the test battery are its wide use and acceptance throughout the country, its Government sponsorship, its avoidance of verbal capacity as the sole basis for measuring I.Q., and its measurement of physical coordination, such as finger and manual dexterity. Its main drawbacks are the time required to administer it (roughly two and one-half hours), the fact that it requires special testing equipment, that test administrators must be trained in the technique, and that it must be administered by employees of a Government agency.

The psychologist and chief test technician for the state employment service recommended setting a minimum I.Q. score of 80 as a passing point on the premise that a lower score would indicate inability to adapt to changing job requirements and a lack of promotional potential. Scores on the dexterity and coordination tests were decided subjectively, and no minimum passing point was set.

Of all applicants invited to take the tests only 53 percent appeared —54 percent of the men and 52 percent of the women. No study was made of why so few appeared, but there could be a number of reasons: fear of a written test, tacit acknowledgment of illiteracy, unwillingness to take a day off from the present job with resulting loss of pay, personal problems such as inability to arrange for a baby sitter or transportation, or simply a lack of sufficient interest in a job at the plant.

Of those who took the tests, 73 percent passed—66 percent of the women and 77 percent of the men. Of the 9,220 who had been invited to take the tests, 34 percent of the women and 41 percent of the men had survived the screening and remained for further consideration in the selection process.

Until July 1964 applicants were interviewed both by a representative of the personnel department and by a line supervisor. Each interview was scheduled for 15 minutes and, usually, two personnel interviewers worked with one supervisor. The personnel interviewers passed approximately 60 percent of the people they interviewed on to the line supervisor, who accepted tentatively about 80 percent of those he interviewed. Thus tentative acceptance was given to 40 to 50 percent of the people who appeared for interviews.

The personnel interviewer followed this schedule:

- 1-2 minutes, put the applicant at ease.
- 4-5 minutes, verify the information on the application; add supplementary data such as date of birth and names of references.
- 4-5 minutes, hold a general discussion with the applicant to determine the value of his experience and estimate his general potential value as an employee.
- 2-3 minutes, explain the hiring procedure, describe working conditions, and answer questions.

The line supervisor spent his interview time telling the applicant, in some detail, what would be expected of him as an employee and evaluating the applicant's ability and desire to perform in his specific production area.

When the interview by the line supervisor was eliminated, the overall selection percentage remained fairly constant (40 to 50 percent), possibly because the personnel interviewer, faced with the responsibility of making the hiring decision, became more selective than he had been when the hiring decision rested with the foreman. This might seem to indicate that the functional interview was not necessary. However, the Dover selection and placement manager did not agree with this conclusion. He pointed out:

> It must be recognized that by the time selections were being made by the personnel interviewers, they had worked closely with the line supervisors for several months. They had learned a good deal about the various operations, and they had learned even more about the personal idiosyncrasies of the supervisors. Thus they were interviewing with more knowledge than would have been the case had there never been the functional interview.
>
> There were also certain subjective values to the functional interview. The supervisors, particularly at the shift foreman level, deeply appreciated that we "cared enough" to consult them in this manner. They also appreciated the fact that when a new worker reported they already knew a good deal about him. This made the break-in period much easier for the foreman as well as the employee.

The selection and placement manager also agreed that there were some negative aspects to the functional interview. The foreman's attention was often divided, since he was primarily responsible for floor production, and he sometimes regarded the time spent in personnel as time wasted. In addition, many tended to be overselective when interviewing candidates for jobs several weeks in advance of the actual personnel needs.

Reference checking was described by the personnel department as "one of the more onerous tasks," but one on which a great deal of emphasis was placed. There were three main problems: only one man in the personnel department was familiar with the Dover area; police were often reluctant to allow access to their files; many people seemed reluctant to talk freely when asked their opinions of others.

Physical examinations resulted in the rejection of only 195 people, 148 of whom were rejected because of an "unstable back" as shown by the back X-ray required of all male candidates for hourly paid jobs.

With regard to the hiring of Negroes, the company let its position as an equal opportunity employer be known early in the game. Informal observations indicated that applications from Negroes were received in about the same proportion as the percentage of Negroes in the population of the area. An ample number of applications was received from Negroes seeking blue-collar jobs, but the plant did not get Negro applicants, either in quantity or quality, for white-collar or professional jobs.

"Our experience in hiring unskilled or semiskilled Negroes has been good," said the selection and placement manager. "Applications have been plentiful; the results of interviews, physicals, and reference checks have not appeared significantly different from those of the white applicants. Turnover statistics seem comparable for both races."

According to a Dover NAACP leader, Negro acceptance of the testing and screening procedure was excellent. Even though the test might be considered discriminatory by some in the sense that culturally disadvantaged persons would be less able to pass than others, the mere fact that GF did use an objective screening device was gratifying to a group which had all too often in the past been limited to subjective evaluation.

Hiring of maintenance craftsmen presented a problem dramatically opposed to the one involved in hiring production workers in that there were not sufficient applicants for the skilled-trade positions. In addition, many applications came from tradesmen who had backgrounds in residential construction and maintenance rather than industrial experience. Many who did qualify had been working at construction wage rates, usually in excess of $4.50 per hour, and were not interested in working at industrial rates, which paid a maximum of $3.00 per hour.

The problem was solved in several ways. Newspaper advertising did attract some applicants from the Wilmington, Baltimore, and Philadelphia areas. Production workers with high mechanical aptitudes were promoted, and men with residential or heavy construction experience were hired and trained. This sometimes made it necessary to hire personnel several weeks in advance of actual need in order to allow for training time. In addition, extra overtime was worked by maintenance personnel, and GF maintenance workers were brought in from other plants on a temporary basis both to accomplish necessary work and to train new employees.

The personnel department was also faced with necessity of hiring for salaried jobs ranging from messenger to research technologist. In the lower grades there were no real problems, and the needs were adequately met. In the higher grades the situation was similar to that with maintenance personnel: there was not a ready supply in the Dover area. Extensive advertising was done in Wilmington, Philadelphia, and Baltimore, and—to a limited extent—in New York City and Washington, D.C. A good salary and fringe benefit package plus the opportunity to work in a new plant were sufficient advantages to attract ample applicants. In some cases, however, the personnel department ran into a reluctance on the part of college recruits and some wives from metropolitan areas to move into the Dover community with its lack of urban amenities.

The following is part of the summary of a report written by the Dover selection and placement manager. It is included here for its value to others who may be faced with similar problems.

> Several of our major problems were mechanical and revolved about the numbers of applications received, the variety of jobs to be filled, and the amount of work that had to be accomplished within a stipulated period. No one, we think, expected to receive 12,000 applications. One of the problems we encountered as a consequence of this avalanche was the establishment of an effective record-keeping system. Our files were set up by broadly defined job areas and applications were filed alphabetically within those classifications. We would recommend that all applications be filed alphabetically in a master file and or cross-referenced to cards filed by job skill. This would make it possible to always find an application in answer to an applicant's query about his status and would make it possible to "multi-file" applications showing a varied background of skills.

We encountered some reluctance on the part of line supervisors to interview for positions that were not to be activated for several weeks or months. As a result, when staffing needs accelerated rapidly, our lead time quickly disappeared and we were forced to eliminate the line supervisor's interview. We would recommend that interviews be commenced as early as possible in the start-up period and continue at an orderly pace. We lost very few applicants because of excessive lead time between the interview and acceptance dates and the actual starting date of employment.

We would recommend that line supervisors be thoroughly trained in the use of the probationary period as a step in the selection procedure. We emphasized this with individual foremen but found that they occasionally were reluctant to terminate unsatisfactory employees. Failure to do this during probation has resulted in a few cases of extreme inconvenience and the maintenance on the payroll of undesirables.

We have also gained more positive knowledge. The functional interview by foremen was extremely valuable. The General Aptitude Test Battery has been and continues to be a most satisfactory screening device. Our general public relations program was—in this rural area—of inestimable value to the employment function. We have done no advertising or other solicitation for any applicants except out-of-town advertising for skilled personnel not available in lower Delaware.

What have we learned? We have learned that from the viewpoint of staffing, projects like this are entirely feasible. We have developed, we think, a smooth and effective screening procedure, and as a consequence of this we have acquired an efficient work force for the Jell-O/Dover plant of General Foods.

PUBLIC RELATIONS AND THE MOVE

Chapter VII

PUBLIC RELATIONS AND THE MOVE

General Foods' decision to close four Jell-O Division plants and consolidate their operations in one new plant created public relations problems in three areas:

1. How to ease the blow, insofar as possible, in the four old towns.
2. How to cope with the inevitable flood of presentations and sales pitches from communities seeking the new plant.
3. How to lay a sound foundation for good relationships with the new community when it was selected.

As to the first of these problems, GF was determined to leave the older communities with the best possible feelings. This the company attempted to do in all four of the old communities. Of course, the major problems were in the two smaller communities—LeRoy and Orange—where the impact of the plant closings would be greatest.

LeRoy had a population of approximately 6,800. The Jell-O plant and four other industries provided employment for about 1,500 people, of which Jell-O had about 350, or 22 percent of the total industrial employment. The plant's annual tax payment of approximately $16,500 was about 2.6 percent of the total tax collection. Local purchases by the plant amounted to approximately \$188,000, while an additional \$208,000 was spent in nearby Batavia.

Orange had a population of about 6,000. The Minute plant and 11 other small industries provided employment for about 925 people, of which Minute had 97, or approximately 10 percent. However, if the adjoining town of Athol was taken into consideration, total industrial employment was 4,250, of which the Minute plant force represented only 2 percent. The plant's annual tax payment of approximately \$22,000 was just under 3 percent of the total tax collection.

However, the economic importance of the plants was not the only consideration. Both plants and their employees also loomed large in the social, cultural, and spiritual life of the communities. They donated money and talent to community projects; employees served in municipal offices, on school boards, and in church offices. In short, they were part and parcel of community life. In addition, both plants were the original "home" of the famous products they made (as was Walter Baker in Dorchester), and the townspeople looked upon them with an almost proprietary interest: the plants were "their" plants. LeRoy without Jell-O and Orange without Minute were unthinkable.

Typical of the feeling toward the GF operations was a full-page testimonial in the LeRoy *Gazette-News* in 1957 when Jell-O celebrated its sixtieth anniversary. Sponsored by 81 local merchants and associations, it read in part:

> For 26 years under the ownership of the Woodward family and 31 years as a part of General Foods, Jell-O has been an important factor in the industrial and community work of LeRoy. To an appreciable degree you have stabilized economic factors in our community and sought with us village betterment along all lines.
>
> You have been a friendly concern. From the ranks you have given us village presidents, village trustees, presidents and members of the Board of Education, a water commissioner, and chairmen of committees seeking local attainments. You have been generous in your support of all our community projects and drives that possessed merit or filled needs.

With this sort of community attitude toward the plants and their employees, plus the economic factor, it is not surprising that GF's announcement of the impending closing was greeted with shock and dismay. "This will ruin us," said the mayor of LeRoy. Newspapers called it a "serious blow." Townspeople were stunned. The news of the LeRoy closing—probably because Jell-O was such a widely known product—was given national distribution by the Associated Press.

In Dorchester and Hoboken, community reaction was considerably different, because the loss of a single plant in these heavily industrialized urban areas was obviously not as serious. In Boston, a very history-conscious area, newspapers played up the loss of a venerable plant which they regarded as one of America's industrial landmarks. The *Boston Herald* said: "The aroma of chocolate that has sweetened the Neponset Valley around Dorchester Lower Mills since before the Revolution will pass into history in two years." The Quincy, Massachusetts, *Patriot-Ledger* remarked: "Aside from the economic angle the closing of the Walter Baker plant involves no little sentiment for an area which cherishes its historical heritage. . . ." Subsequent stories in Boston-area newspapers did mention the fact that the plant employed approximately 800 people and that many would probably choose to stay in the Dorchester area rather than move to the new plant.

In New Jersey the press was even more casual in its treatment of the news that the Hoboken plant would be closed. In fact, there was a significant absence of municipal handwringing in Hoboken during the entire shutdown period.

Thus it was immediately obvious that GF should concentrate its principal efforts on LeRoy and Orange and, perhaps to some extent, in the Dorchester area. Consequently, most of the company's efforts in Dorchester and Hoboken should properly be termed employee relations rather than public or community relations.

One of the first steps in LeRoy and Orange was to arrange meetings between town officials and the operations manager of the Jell-O Division, who had headed the task force which had recommended closing the four plants. He was able to explain in depth the compelling reasons for the planned consolidation and the reasons GF probably would not build the consolidated plant in either of the two towns. He also made it clear that the company would do all in its power to be helpful in a practical way. First, the company would underwrite the cost of an industrial survey in each of the communities. Secondly, it would actively seek buyers for the plants, with the hope that replacement industry would provide jobs for terminated employees.

These initial steps did a great deal to alter the attitude of people in both communities. This is evidenced by the following paragraph in an editorial in the LeRoy *Gazette-News:*

> With the passing of days and official conferences with Jell-O executives, there has gradually developed a calmer understanding of the motivating reasons. Jell-O has accepted the expressions of regret by LeRoy as being an honest appreciation and tribute of our community feeling toward the company. It has been gratifying to them, and they in turn have indicated their desire to cooperate with us in seeking advantageous disposal of the modern manufacturing building for future industrial use. . . .

Something of the same air of calmness and understanding was also returning to Orange. There the *Enterprise and Journal* editorialized:

> Whenever a large corporation such as General Foods . . . buys smaller industrial plants in an area, it is a natural economic fact that, sooner or later, consolidation of these plants becomes necessary.
>
> True, every consideration will be given employees of the company, both in job opportunities at the new plant or in adequate separation pay. But the fact remains that the primary interest of the company must of necessity be with the company, and not with the town in which it is located.

As for the industrial survey which GF was underwriting for Orange, the newspaper commented:

> Orange is about to learn all about itself. The survey just began by the Fantus Area Research Company will be coldly analytical. There will be no overemphasis on good points and no disguising of bad points. . . . This is the kind of examination and analysis that every industrial town and city needs.

Two other steps proved to be of significant value in bringing about a change of attitude in the two towns. First, the local plant managers kept city officials informed of all developments at the same time as they were announced to employees. In addition, all of the "On the Move" bulletins were given to the local press. There were few news releases. Newsmen used the bulletins as a basis for their own stories, which often included statements which the company would not ordinarily have put into news releases.

Important, too, was the fact that the plants and employees continued their participation in community affairs right up to the day the doors closed. News stories about various grants and donations frequently noted the fact that these contributions were continuing even though the plant was scheduled to close.

When the LeRoy plant finally shut down in July 1964, the community attitude was in great contrast to the fear of impending doom, the shock, and the dismay expressed in March 1962. GF people had reason to believe that their efforts to be fair and helpful had been effective when they read these words in the local newspaper:

> To you, the functioning executives, the department heads, and to the workers who are accompanying you to the new plant at Dover or remaining in LeRoy, we are saying: "Farewell Jell-O, but not our goodbye," for Jell-O and your other products are going to continue in our homes along with the warm memories of the men and women who for over half a century made Jell-O such a vital and beneficial part of LeRoy.

Although Orange had to say goodbye to the Minute Rice and Tapioca operation, it did not see the immediate shutdown of the plant. In March 1964, before the transfer to Dover had been completed, the Jell-O Division decided to continue operating the Orange plant to produce test-market quantities of some experimental products and to provide additional packaging capabilities for products made in other plants. Approximately 35 employees were kept on the payroll.*

The lesson to be learned from this review of what GF tried to do with respect to its relationships with communities it found itself obliged to leave is simply this: let a company conduct itself in an open, forthright way, communicating with the city officials, the press, and local businessmen promptly and fully just as it does with its own employees. And let this flow of information come from the local plant manager. Once such a basis of confidence has been established, the community is better able to withstand the shock of shutdown, especially if the announcement of intent is made with plenty of lead time before the doors will actually close.

But there is more to it than that. There should be practical proposals and action on the part of the company to help the municipality try to find a new employer to take over the plant and thus keep employment and tax levels sustained. There is an element of self-interest in this, but when it is accompanied by a sincere desire to help the community

*In January 1966 the Orange plant was, in fact, still operating, and employment was about at pre-move levels.

"sell itself" by such means as offering to provide area research studies, then it becomes evidence of a genuine commitment to help put the vacated house in order. Closer to home, of course, is the demonstration by the company of its concern for its employees who are unable to transfer. Helping them to find other employment is the answer; and the more effective this is, the more the word gets around. By the measure of the acceptance and discharge of its social responsibilities a company is judged by the community involved in a shutdown operation. It is not judged by what it says but by what it does.

Solving the Second Problem

A second problem which involved GF's public relations people was created by the March 8, 1962, press release which announced that the four plants would be closed and that GF was seeking a site for a new plant. The news release specifically stated that the company was looking for a 50-acre site in a community located within 250 miles of New York City.

While the company knew that its policy of advance information to employees and communities would inevitably involve it in solicitations and presentations from many a zealous chamber of commerce, it did not anticipate the deluge that resulted. GF's headquarters was inundated with telephone calls, telegrams, and visits from various municipal delegations. Some groups attempted to bypass the Jell-O Division and carry their appeals to top corporate officers.

Many communities had logical presentations which were deserving of the company's serious consideration. But some of the appeals were from communities which obviously did not fit the company's well-publicized requirements. A few were obviously politically inspired; others were little more than publicity stunts.

Perhaps the most ingenious of all the serious presentations came for Amsterdam, New York, where a civic club sparked a letter-writing campaign. As a result, GF received approximately 3,000 letters from Amsterdam citizens, each enclosing a box top or label from some GF product and urging Jell-O to locate the new plant in their city. Although the campaign did not bring the desired results, it did get nationwide publicity and compliments from GF's top management. Each of the 3,000 letter writers received the following reply from the general manager of the Jell-O Division:

Dear Rooter-for-Amsterdam:

You will readily understand why I am turning to a form letter to answer you—and thousands of others—who impressed us, and swamped our mail room, by your enthusiastic advocacy of Amsterdam for our new plant site. Amsterdam is certainly a get-up-and-go city, and your ingenious campaign was a first rate marketing stroke. Coming from a company that prides itself on its marketing, I hope you will take that as the compliment it is meant to be.

If get-up-and-go were the prime requisite, Amsterdam would now be high on our list. But while an alert, active community is an important consideration, we must also consider a host of other questions which our engineers, traffic experts, and marketing specialists have been studying for months. Some of the broad conclusions of the studies are already in; and rather than encourage false hopes, we must tell you that they rule strongly against Amsterdam's possibilities.

Thank you for the trouble you took to write us; and while this letter may be disappointing, I hope you will believe that we will always have a warm spot in our hearts for a city that surely knows how to speak up for itself.

Letters came in to GF by the hundreds from chambers of commerce, mayors, city officials, and, in some cases, national political leaders writing on behalf of their constituencies. All of these received personal replies which in most cases were designed to discourage false hopes and further solicitation of the company. In effect, they said: "Don't call us; we'll call you."

Although the early announcement of its intentions to build a new plant created—briefly—an almost chaotic situation, GF remained convinced that the advantages in terms of employee and community goodwill far outweighed any annoyance or inconvenience. After all, an organization geared to the movement of 14 million packages of food per day was certainly equipped to deal courteously and patiently with all comers, and in such a way as to prevent any falloff of consumer acceptance for its products.

Laying a Sound Foundation

GF's efforts to get acquainted in Dover began as soon as the company announced in May 1962 that the Delaware capital was one of the leading places being considered as the site for the new plant. Doverites, generally, were overjoyed by the announcement, as what community wouldn't be when told it was likely to be the site of a new multimillion-dollar industry whose plant and products would be assets to the eyes and pocketbook. The editor and publisher of Dover's *Delaware State News* wrote the following day:

> The best news Dover has had in many a year broke yesterday.
>
> The fact that General Foods Corporation is seriously considering this area as the location for their best and most modern plant is the kind of a break that comes only once in a generation.
>
> I was one of the group that sat in with the key officials of this outstanding food processing company to hear the official announcement that they are seriously considering Dover.
>
> And I am quite sure they mean business—otherwise they wouldn't announce their intentions in this manner. Their program seems clear. They have announced it to their employees in a March 8 release when they indicated that they would be consolidating their four outmoded plants. And the information disclosed yesterday was also given to their employees.
>
> Their concern with the kind of facilities the City of Dover can supply is perfectly legitimate.
>
> But I have no doubts that all these requirements can be met. It may not be easy, but certainly an industry with 1,200 employees deserves extra special consideration.

It was approximately three and a half months before GF could announce that its selection of Dover was definite and final. During this period there were numerous contacts between GF executives, city officials, and civic leaders.

Working relationships were established with the local newspapers and radio stations. Two newspapers served the area: the *Delaware State News,* which was published in Dover, was highly oriented to local news coverage; its circulation at that time was approximately 11,500. Also circulated in Dover were the two papers published in Wilmington: the *Morning News* had a circulation of approximately 32,000, while the *Evening Journal's* circulation was approximately 73,000. The two papers maintained a bureau in Dover, and each ran a daily one- or two-page section devoted to news from the lower part of the state. Dover also had two radio stations, both of which covered local news events.

During the period from May 15 to September 5, 1962, while many factors bearing on the selection of Dover were being explored, there was little to tell the press and radio stations. GF's public relations people really swung into action the week before the board of directors' meeting when the final decision on Dover was to be made. In anticipation of a favorable decision, full preparations were made to rush the story to employees and the press. This involved preparing a bulletin from the chairman to the organization, a letter from the general manager of the Jell-O Division to employees in the four old plants, a general press release, and a special press release keyed to the Dover area. Packages of letters with attached press releases were sent to the four plants by car to insure that they would be on hand when the green light was given. The special releases were carried to Dover for delivery to the press there, and appropriate GF executives were alerted to be in Dover to convey the news personally to the governor, mayor, city manager, and other officials. Also on hand at Dover were supplies of supplementary material, such as annual reports, a fact booklet on the company, and photographs of principal officers and executives.

In addition, all GF public relations outlets were supplied with a list of questions that were likely to be asked when the story broke, and the answers to them, so that the supplementary information given out would be as complete as possible. The list included such questions as:

- Where is the site?
- What did the land cost and from whom was it purchased?
- How big will the plant be? What will it cost?
- How many employees? How many transferred? How many were hired locally?
- How much will the annual payroll be?
- Why was Dover chosen?
- Why is the company consolidating four apparently prosperous plants?
- Where does the company stand on unions? On integration?

Included in the special Dover press release was warm praise for the community and for officials of both city and state. The Jell-O Division general manager was quoted as saying:

> Dover meets our basic operating requirements most satisfactorily. It is near ocean shipping for importation of raw materials and is centrally located in the large Eastern market for shipment of our many products. Importantly, too, Dover offers attractive living conditions and pleasant surroundings for our employees.

Jell-O's facilities improvement manager, who had been working with Dover officials and was by now well known in the community, was also quoted in the release:

> Day in and day out, over a period of many weeks, these men have responded promptly to our requests for a great variety of information and have come forward to aid us in working out the many details that are necessarily involved in a project of this magnitude.
>
> I know that on many occasions they have put aside other pressing matters and have sacrificed their own personal time to furnish necessary facts and information on which we could base our decisions.

The *Delaware State News* used type two inches high to announce that Jell-O was coming to Dover. The Wilmington papers were a bit more restrained, but it was page-one news all the way. All three newspapers carried glowing editorial welcomes within the next few days.

Within two days after the announcement in Dover, GF was host to Chamber of Commerce officials at a breakfast, state officials at a luncheon, and city officials at a dinner. On hand to meet these officials were the general manager and operations manager of the Jell-O Division, plus several men who would hold executive positions at the new plant. In planning these affairs, there was one important guideline: make them good, but do not go overboard. As a result, all the initial affairs—as well as many subsequent ones over the next two years—were conducted in a relaxed and informal manner.

Prior to breaking ground for the new plant, GF arranged the initial contact between city and state officials and top company executives. Delaware's governor and secretary of state; Dover's mayor, city manager, and Chamber of Commerce president; and several newsmen were flown to White Plains for a tour of the GF Kitchens and luncheon with GF's chairman and other top executives.

Little time was lost in getting the new plant construction under way. Ground-breaking ceremonies were held on October 18, 1962, with the customary silver-plated shovels—donated for the occasion by a Dover merchant—wielded by the GF chairman, the governor, and the mayor.

For the next several months, just about everything that occurred with respect to GF and the new plant made headlines in the local newspapers: the naming of the plant manager and members of his staff, progress on construction, the city's plans for a temporary access road to the plant and the state's plans for permanent improvements to

Dover's highway network, and a host of other items. Editorial comment continued to be highly favorable; and if there was any undercurrent of dissatisfaction, it was not apparent.

In May 1963 the Jell-O Division published in the Dover newspaper the first of a series of institutional advertisements. The first was a progress report to the community. It read, in part:

> Work on the plant structure should be pretty well finished by late fall. Then will come the extensive job of transferring manufacturing lines from our present plants, on a process-by-process basis, and installing new equipment over a period of at least a year. So production startups will extend from this November through most of next year. Accordingly, job opportunities will become available over this long period.
>
> We feel highly complimented that more than 2,100 men and women have registered interest in working for us since our temporary Dover office was opened last October. Now we are prepared to receive applications. . . .
>
> Now that spring is here, many General Foods people working at the four plants to be consolidated at Jell-O/Dover—and their families—are taking advantage of the fine weather to visit Dover. They're exploring housing possibilities, schools, churches, and all the other things that are important to folks considering a big move.
>
> GF people who visit Dover are deeply impressed with the friendliness and cooperation they meet on all sides—whether their contacts are with members of the state or city government, business and professional men and women, clergy, educators, or Doverites they just meet in stores or on the street. The warm and sincere reception Dover gave General Foods was an important consideration in our decision to build the big new plant here. You can be sure that it's also one of the biggest reasons why we're looking forward with genuine pleasure to becoming a business citizen of this fine city.

This first GF advertisement in the local newspaper brought the following editorial comment the next day:

> This report only continues to strengthen a conviction that this outfit seems to do things right. Of course, the first right thing they did was to decide to locate their great new plant in Dover, Delaware. Every move since that memorable announcement has been proper. Officials of the company have been efficient, courteous, and friendly. I've observed with admiration the way they have taken care of their employees. They have kept them fully informed, advised them of the reasons for the move, given them every possible help in

> making a choice. And if the decision has been to go along, GF has really done everything possible to smooth the move.
>
> In the report yesterday glowing reference was made to the friendliness and cooperation extended on the part of our citizens. We are glad GF is finding it this way. . . . At the same time I feel I can speak for the people of Dover and of all Delaware in saying—"We like you, too."

The above is typical of the atmosphere of cordiality in which GF operated during its first few months in Dover. Obviously, the community had a general feeling of enthusiasm as it realized its potential for growth and prosperity brought about in part by the new plant. As the steel and concrete began to rise and more GF people moved to Dover, the company employed a native Doverite, a former newspaperman with experience in public relations, as community relations manager for the plant.

This proved to be a good move in several ways. Many people in the community were gratified that the company assigned a local person to a staff-level position at the new plant. Moreover, it broadened GF's range of contacts with local people and gave them the feeling that they were dealing with a person who was "one of us" rather than with someone who had only recently arrived on the scene. But, perhaps most important of all, the assignment of a plant community relations manager took the responsibility for local public relations off the shoulders of other staff members who were engaged in the herculean task of getting the new plant into operation.

There was an intense community and area curiosity about the company and the new plant, which GF did its best to satisfy, using several other means in addition to institutional advertising and news releases.

Dozens of talks, product displays, and film showings were presented before club groups throughout a wide area around Dover. These appearances provided an excellent opportunity to present GF's history and background and some of its philosophies of conducting business; to familiarize the public with the company's many products, particularly those to be made in Dover; and to go into detail about the size, complexity, capacity, and construction of the new plant. One great advantage of such a speaking program is that it gives the public, or at least a large and influential segment, a chance for a face-to-face meeting with a representative of the company and an opportunity to ask questions. Another benefit, of course, is that almost all such meetings result in news stories in local papers.

Community interest in the plant also brought many requests for guided tours before the plant went into production. All such requests were politely turned down, with the explanation that it was not safe to have groups in the building while construction and equipment installation were under way. However, all were told that a public open house would be held when the plant was in full operation.

State and city officials as well as the press were kept aware of progress during the construction and start-up phases. Periodic tours were arranged for the governor and other state officials; the mayor, city council members, city manager, city engineer, and so forth; and various groups of newsmen. Usually, these tours were made in small groups of eight to ten persons, with the operations manager acting as the principal guide. Frequently the tour was followed by an informal luncheon or dinner at a nearby inn. These tours enabled the state and city officials to talk with some authority about the plant in their many public contacts. Press tours almost always resulted in favorable features, columns, or radio comment.

Another opportunity for reaching a sizable segment of the community was an annual "Home and Trade Show" sponsored by the local Chamber of Commerce. This was used primarily as a means of familiarizing the public with GF products. The company participated in the show for the first two years it was in the community; it used large product displays furnished by the GF Kitchens in White Plains. These displays were always manned by persons qualified to answer questions about the company, the plant, and the products.

The Douglas Williams survey report, made in the summer of 1962, touched upon some situations in the Dover area which could have become problems in community relations had they been ignored.

One was the community attitude toward integration. The Williams report had concluded that integration in the Dover area was proceeding slowly but smoothly; that almost everyone looked upon it as an inevitable development, but that some resented it deeply. GF made clear to the community the company's established position as an equal-opportunity employer. Company spokesmen did not go around shouting this position from the rooftops, but neither did they hesitate to give a complete and clear answer when asked. In addition, the operations manager, personnel manager, and community relations manager made early contact with Negro leaders in the community for the purpose of discussing mutual problems. There were no "incidents" of any kind, and very little—if any—community reaction to GF's policy. Apparently, townspeople simply accepted it as part of the inevitable move toward integration.

The Williams report also concluded that GF people should not "push" their way into community affairs. They should be willing to serve but should wait to be asked. All of the plant staff people were aware of the Williams recommendation and—aside from joining in church activities and a few transfers into fraternal and service groups—none leaped into community activities.

On its side, the community was quick to realize that the plant provided a large pool of talent that it could utilize. Within a short time many GF people had been asked to join such activities as the United Community Fund, the local hospital's board of directors, the Chamber of Commerce board, a citizen's advisory committee for the local schoools, the Boy Scouts, boy's baseball leagues, and numerous civic and service clubs. One transferred employee had been elected to the council of a nearby small town after campaigning on the promise that, even though he was a newcomer, he was as interested in the welfare and progress of his new home town as he had been in his old home town.

The Williams survey, in questioning Dover area people regarding their attitude on unions, had found that many were anti-union by inclination but had no strong feelings on the matter because of relatively little exposure to unions. By the time the unions began their drive to organize the plant employees, the townspeople—particularly key civic leaders and businessmen—were more aware of the issue, and many felt that a successful organizing drive at the plant would spark a drive to organize other businesses in the community.

The company's position was based upon a long-standing policy which was, in essence, that all employees were free to choose representatives for collective bargaining but that no employee would be required to join or not to join any organization. In other words, employees could be represented by a union if a majority so desired, but there would be no union shop.

When the unions petitioned the National Labor Relations Board for recognition as bargaining agents, a company news release was issued stating the facts contained in the petitions, pointing out that the company had had excellent relationships with the two unions in the past, and stating the company's position with respect to union organization. Until the NLRB election three weeks later, the press was kept informed of all developments and was given the text of the plant operations manager's letter to employees which was issued about a week before the election.

During this period three editorials appeared in the Dover newspaper. All three urged employees to vote against union representation. These were accompanied by several letters to the editor which were also predominantly anti-union. Following the election, which the union won by a large majority, the newspaper editor and various businessmen expressed surprise and concern at the results. However, the newspaper pointed out that a majority of those who voted in the election were newly hired local people. There had been relatively few transferees from the older plants up to that time. The community as a whole apparently paid but scant attention to the union election. There was no outburst of letters to the editor, and the entire matter died quickly.

The Amalgamated Food and Allied Workers Union, which represented the majority of the employees, spontaneously expressed its attitude toward the company and the plant consolidation some months later. At the plant dedication union officials presented GF's chairman with a plaque which read:

> On the occasion of your dedication of the Jell-O/Dover plant, we employees—members of Local 56—with a feeling of pride do hereby wish you a most successful operation knowing that in your success also lies our guarantee for a bright future.

The final—and biggest—task in the process of introducing GF in Dover was planning and conducting a dedication and open house. Here the company's experience with such affairs at its San Leandro, California, plant and its White Plains headquarters proved invaluable. Checklists and scrapbooks from these events provided a model for the Dover ceremonies. Planning for the affair began nearly a year in advance.

The time selected, May 4 to 8, 1965, was several months after the plant was finally completed and in full operation. The delay in holding the dedication was due primarily to a desire to avoid holding the affair during the winter, but this also gave plant personnel an opportunity for a thorough shakedown of equipment and operating procedures before opening the doors to the public. The schedule of events shaped up as follows:

May 4. Press preview—30 or 40 invited guests from newspapers, radio, and trade publications were given a plant tour followed by dinner.

May 5. Dedication—GF's board of directors and wives, Jell-O Division executives, state and city officials, executives of other Delaware industries were invited for luncheon and a plant tour.

May 6. Employee Family Day—estimated 5,000 to 6,000 visitors.

May 7. 140 community leaders invited for a tour and lunch; open house for public from 2:00 to 9:00 P.M. Estimated 5,000 visitors.

May 8. (Saturday.) Public open house from 10:00 A.M. to 5:00 P.M. Estimated 5,000 visitors.

The first step in planning was the preparation of objectives and a schedule of events for the five-day period plus detailed checklists for each day. The master checklist included such items as the following:

1. Determining the objective—to dedicate the new plant and foster employee and community understanding and goodwill.
2. Selecting the date—so as to avoid conflict with other community events and allow ample time for preparation.
3. Drawing up the guest list—to include present employees and their families, retired employees, stockholders, business leaders, brokers and dealers in company products, civic officials, school superintendents and teachers, clergy, labor leaders, club and organization leaders, press and radio, and the community at large.
4. Sending out invitations—that is, personalized cards or letters to specific groups or a letter from the plant manager; newspaper ads and radio announcements for public.
5. Providing suitable transportation and parking.
6. Holding the actual reception—seeing that guests were welcomed by plant management representative; that there was desk for information and the handing out of any printed material and identification badges.
7. Providing souvenirs—such as a booklet with a welcome by the plant manager, a picture story of plant operations, a diagram of the tour route, facts about company and plant, and a product package for adults and a special memento for children.
8. Conducting the plant tour—which included selecting a tour route which would aid the visitor's understanding of the manufacturing process, create the least interference with production and safety, avoid bottlenecks or retracing steps, and keep an even flow of visitors through plant. Arranging direction markers, painted aisle lines or tape, safety barriers, simple descriptive signs for equipment, factual signs about production, and economic facts on how plant benefits community. Providing a rest area if tour were lengthy.

9. Setting up exhibits—if possible showing raw materials and steps to finished product; charts or diagrams of operations not seen by visitors; products made at other company plants; plant safety program, employee benefits, etc.
10. Serving refreshments—in plant cafeteria if possible; if not, using tent or other protected area.
11. Attending to service to the press—such as preparing a complete press kit and seeing that newsmen had access to management personnel.
12. Providing a follow-up—mailing souvenirs to important guests who were unable to attend and thank-you letters to press, radio, civic officials, and all others who participated in any special activities.

Once the schedule of events was in final form, attention turned to detailed lists for each day of the planned dedication and open house. No detail, however minor, was left to chance. Each item on the lists was specifically assigned to one person who was expected to see that his or her responsibility was planned, coordinated with other activities, and carried out.

One of the problems was the selection of a tour route for the public. Like many other plants, Jell-O/Dover had not been built with visitors in mind, and it was difficult to select a route which showed the scope of the plant's operations but at the same time was not too lengthy. All visitors were kept on the ground floor to eliminate crowding on stairways with the safety hazards such a prospect would present. Since a tour route that covered all the processing and packaging areas, even if restricted to the first floor, would have been excessively long, some areas had to be left out. A major area eliminated from the tour was the one for chocolate processing. To compensate for this, an exhibit was set up to show graphically the entire chocolate-making process.

An "Open House Coordinating Committee" was set up under the direction of the plant manager. It included representatives from all major plant divisions—community relations, personnel, manufacturing, engineering, and maintenance—as well as representatives from each of the production areas on the tour route. This committee concerned itself primarily with the preparation of the plant for visitors—painting, cleanup, clearance of the tour route, and so on—and with problems involved in keping production lines supplied with packaging materials without using aisles assigned to the tour route. It also had the task of arranging production schedules so that all equipment on the route would be operating during the hours that visitors were expected to be in the plant.

The public open house at Dover required a "free flow" type of tour, since it was obviously impossible to set up guided trips through the plant for the several thousand expected visitors. This meant that the tour route had to be well marked with directional signs, have safety ropes and barriers, and be well supplied with informational signs. Production superintendents in the various departments were extremely helpful in planning signs to explain the operation of the equipment and the amounts of product that each line was capable of turning out in a day, week, month, or year. More than 200 such signs were placed along the tour route. More than 35 men from the various departments and from research, quality control, production planning, and engineering were stationed along the tour route to explain various operations, answer questions, keep visitors at a safe distance from equipment, and keep traffic flowing. These guides wore red "hard hats." A sign at the tour entrance read, "If you have questions, ask the men in the red hats."

A member of the management staff of the plant was stationed at the tour entrance to greet all guests. Immediately inside the tour entrance was a desk where girls from the plant office handed each visitor a souvenir booklet. The tour route was laid out so that it ended at a point convenient to the visitor parking area. And since it was not feasible to use the plant cafeteria for serving refreshments, a large tent was erected at the exit point for this purpose.

A rundown of the day-to-day activities may prove valuable to those planning a similar affair:

1. Press preview. Press, radio, and television invited by personal letter from the corporate manager of public relations; press kits supplied by mail to all several days in advance; all visitors given personal attention of members of plant staff and corporate public relations people; tours of plant made in small groups—each group accompanied by one person from production or engineering and by a representative of public relations staff; tours followed by press conference with entire plant management staff available for questioning; informal reception and dinner held at local country club.
2. Dedication. Company officials included several members of the board of directors, officers, and wives; chartered buses transported important guests from airport to plant; special guests included state and city officials, top officers or representatives of

other Delaware industries; brief dedication ceremonies with GF president presiding and unveiling of plaque by GF chairman; reception and luncheon at nearby inn; tours for all guests conducted by plant management staff using motorized carts.

3. Employee Family Day. First of three "open house" days . . . plant open for free-flow tours from 10:00 A.M. to 2:00 P.M. and from 4:00 P.M. to 9:00 P.M. to allow employees on all shifts to bring family.
4. Community Leaders' Day. Local officials, civic leaders, and businessmen invited for tour at 10:00 A.M.; free-flow tour used with special attention to certain guests; reception and luncheon at nearby inn; plant opened to public from 2:00 P.M. to 9:00 P.M.
5. Public Open House. Plant open for tours from 10:00 A.M. to 5:00 P.M.

Jell-O's introduction of its new plant to the Dover community turned out to be a solid success. More than 16,000 people toured the plant during the three days of open house. The local newspaper published a 20-page special section devoted to GF and the new plant. And in the days following the open house plant officials received dozens of letters commenting favorably on the affair. Most people noted the orderliness and cleanliness of the plant; others were obviously impressed with its size and complexity; and still others were amazed at the volume of products it could produce. However, the letter that pleased plant officials most was one that ended with the line, "Thank you for coming to Dover."

AN ASSESSMENT OF THE PROJECT

Chapter VIII

AN ASSESSMENT OF THE PROJECT

The chairman of General Foods, Charles G. Mortimer, dedicated the Jell-O/Dover Plant on May 5, 1965, to "the people we are continually striving to satisfy and please—American homemakers everywhere."

And, speaking at the dedication ceremony, GF President C. W. Cook said:

> This newest addition to General Foods' nationwide network of processing plants represents a sizable investment in time, talent, and dollars. It also incorporates some of the physical facilities of the four plants it replaces and enables us to put today's technology to work on tomorrow's problems and provides us with room to grow and produce—as we already are doing—products not even in existence at the time we decided to move to Dover.
>
> This consolidation is not merely a matter of bringing together the thousands of pieces of machinery, the miles of pipes and wires, the tanks and storage bins, the conveyor belts and all the other

> hardware of the business. This move also involves the far more important gathering together in Dover of people with know-how, with the will and abilities to operate this highly complex plant. We are fortunate that some 500 employees followed their jobs to Dover, and equally fortunate in attracting skilled people locally.

Thus ended the final chapter in the story of Jell-O's move to Dover. The new plant was completed, fully staffed, and in production. Almost all employees who had transferred from the four old plants were happy with their new jobs and with their new home, and most of the local people who had found jobs in the new plant considered themselves fortunate. The community's attitude toward GF and Jell-O/Dover was still extremely favorable. Now, perhaps, was the time to look back upon what had been done, to assess the entire project in terms of what had been important and well done, what had been not so important or not so well done, and what—if anything—might have been left undone.

This had been the timetable:

1960: A task force begins a broad study of all Jell-O Division production facilities.

July 1961: The task force completes its work and recommends that Jell-O's four Eastern plants be combined into a single plant. The division creates a facilities improvement group to continue the study.

February 1962: The facilities improvement group study reinforces the findings of the task force. Jell-O prepares to present its case to the board of directors and requests funds for preliminary engineering.

March 1962: The board agrees, funds are appropriated, and employees are told of the plan to move to some as-yet-undesignated site.

September 1962: Jell-O selects Dover, Delaware, as the site for the new consolidated plant.

October 1962: Ground is broken for the new plant. Offices are opened in Dover.

November 1963: Plant offices are occupied. Transferring employees begin to move to Dover.

January 1964: First production lines are placed in operation on Jell-O gelatin dessert and Log Cabin syrup.

May 1965: Plant is officially dedicated and an open house is held.

No one except the people who were involved in the events of those five years could adequately assess the good points and bad points. The following, then, are the summarized comments of many GF people who were involved in the project, some during the entire five years and some who worked on only certain phases of the project. Opinions were solicited from a large number of people, all of whom were involved in some management or supervisory position which would allow them to see the move in broad perspective. Insofar as possible, the assessments are discussed under the headings of the previous chapters in this book.

An Idea Takes Shape

When a company is faced with the problem of an obsolete plant, it should look carefully at all alternatives before deciding upon a course of action. Initial studies, however, should concentrate upon the most important question—that is, how best to effect major cost reductions and improve profits while providing for future growth and expansion. Refinements of the study and the "how, when, where" details can come later.

During the early phases of the study it is important to keep channels of communication open with top management. Early approval will assure that the study is proceeding in accordance with its wishes. It is also important that management be aware of the disadvantages as well as the advantages inherent in moving. For example, GF was considering a multiple plant consolidation which would result in putting most of its production eggs in one basket with respect to several important products; thus it had to weigh the dangers of a possible work stoppage at the proposed new plant. Management should also know the assumptions upon which conclusions are based and should have a good idea of the accuracy of the financial conclusions.

Early studies can benefit from the use of top talent throughout the entire corporation, at least on a consulting basis. On the other hand, the more people who know of possible plant shutdowns, the greater the chance for news leaks and rumors and possible serious effects on employee morale at the old plants. In GF's case—and this is likely to be so in other cases—it was impossible to do a meaningful study without involving some management and supervisory people from the four old plants. However, the "need to know" criteria should be applied in deciding who should be told of the studies under way.

Even though early studies may indicate the desirability of building a new plant, there will naturally be some opposition to the closing of old plants. Such opposition may be based on sentiment rather than fact or upon the often present tendency to resist change. On the other hand, there are those who want to jump on the bandwagon in favor of the move on the theory that the new is always better than the old. Neither sentiment should be allowed to affect a logical examination of the facts and figures on which the decision must be based.

An important incentive to those engaged in the studies and planning was management's assurance that those who made significant contributions and recommendations would be given the opportunity and the responsibility of carrying out their ideas at the new plant. This also acted to discourage overly optimistic planning since the planner was always acutely aware that he would eventually be responsible for the functions he was planning.

The Idea Becomes a Plan

In proceeding from a feasibility study to actual planning, it is desirable to drop the task force method and set up an organizational unit which can devote its full time and talent to the project. This unit should work on verifying or rejecting the recommendations of the task force and should not get sidetracked into looking at other alternatives.

If a corporation has an engineering service group, the facilities improvement group, or whatever it is called, can be kept small since it can call upon the specialized talent in the engineering group for much of the detailed work that must be done.

Refining the cost and savings estimates will require developing a preliminary plant layout, flow charts, manning tables, and so on. This phase of the work can be vastly simplified if *no* new and untried equipment is considered. However, it is a mistake to assume that this limitation can be continued. In GF's case some of the equipment layouts from the old plants were unworkable in the new plant. Additionally, processing changes, new product introductions, and the opportunity for improvements in efficiency, sanitation, and housekeeping all dictated the introduction of some new equipment. However, this can be done during the preliminary engineering phase of the project.

If prospects for management approval look good, it may be desirable to begin work on some problems which would be expected to arise during preliminary engineering. For example, research testing and approval of proposed processing changes could begin since such changes might be introduced even should management not approve the move to a new plant.

Selecting the Site

The use of an experienced site selection or industrial research firm is desirable. Such firms have more knowledge of locations and experience to draw upon than most companies possess—plus experienced engineers, economists, traffic experts, and so forth to interpret the facts and figures. Had GF done its own site selection, it is possible that the new plant would have been built in a larger city since a more casual look at the figures seems to favor an urban area. Actually, Dover had several advantages over nearby urban areas.

After the new plant site is selected—at least tentatively—a follow-up community survey will give the company a better understanding of any problems it may face. This is particularly valuable when the plan calls for building and staffing a large plant in a small community. Such a survey reveals community attitudes, habits, and prejudices which might differ greatly from those of employees the company will transfer to the new plant. Also, it can be used to give a better indication of labor availability and the degree of desire to work in the new plant.

Even though the community survey showed Dover very receptive to GF, there were a few residents who had negative feelings about the expense of providing necessary utility services for the new plant. Some of these—and they were only a few—were older persons or retired people who oppose any type of tax increase. Additionally, as in many other small and historic towns, there was supposed to be an "old guard"—generally referred to as Old Doverites—who resisted industry, modernization, and change. No such opposition developed, and this might well be true in a similar situation elsewhere. Reports of such opposition are sometimes more fiction than fact.

During the process of deciding upon Dover as the plant site, there was extremely close cooperation between Jell-O and corporate engineering representatives and Dover City officials. These contacts were highly important since GF had to be assured that the city could and would meet the company's requirement. In addition, this proved to be an excellent way to break the ice in the new community since, in many cases, the company people involved became key people on the new plant staff.

Designing, Engineering, and Building the New Plant

There is no substitute for adequate staff planning before beginning construction and during the construction phase. Assembling the Dover plant staff at Port Chester, New York (near GF headquarters), prior to moving to Dover allowed everyone involved to take part in the basic planning. It put the staff in a good position to confer with some of the top corporate talent on special problems. If anything, it might have been desirable to have had even more time for planning some phases of the project.

Few companies are staffed to design and engineer a plant as large and complex as Jell-O/Dover with its 20 acres of floor space and many production lines. Thus most would find it necessary to retain outside engineering assistance. Care should be taken to find a well-qualified, well-staffed organization, preferably one with experience in designing and engineering similar types of plants. The firm selected should have adequately staffed office facilities reasonably near the corporate offices. There are some advantages to employing an engineer-contractor firm for the entire project.

The critical path method, which GF used to control construction and the move of administrative functions and production lines, proved to be highly effective. There is an often overlooked advantage of the critical path method: in order to set it up, someone—in GF's case, the new plant staff and corporate engineering—*has* to think about the thousands of things that must be done, in what manner they should be done, and how long it will take to accomplish each step. Ultimately, everyone involved begins to see the total picture and to know almost instinctively how a delay in a particular step will affect the entire project.

Plant and equipment layout decisions are vastly simplified by the use of models which make it easier to see how each production line will look. Models also make it possible to bring production people—who might find it difficult to understand regular drawings—into the planning process. Frequently, experienced production personnel can spot potential trouble spots which might elude engineers. Precision scale models of very complex installations, while expensive, are also valuable.

Construction began on the Jell-O/Dover plant with approximately 10 percent of final engineering completed. There were some obvious disadvantages in this. Estimating costs and schedules was risky; many changes were necessary after construction began; engineering costs were higher, and cost control was more difficult. In this case there were offsetting advantages. If construction had waited for the completion of engineering, there would have been a one-year delay in realizing cost savings, needed expansion of certain facilities, and utilization of new and improved equipment. The early start of construction may have increased the total project cost to some extent, but this was far outweighed by the advantages realized.

There should be clearly drawn lines of responsibility in the organization set up by the company to handle the project as well as in that of the engineer-contractor. The Jell-O/Dover project was frequently complicated by the division of responsibility between the Jell-O Division and corporate engineering, and by a similar situation arising from the fact that the contractor handled the job from a branch office. Of course, the project could not have been accomplished without the work of the corporate engineering department. However, it would seem desirable to have the department act in an engineering service capacity to the division that has the final responsibility of starting up and operating the plant.

In retrospect, it would seem that GF should have drawn more heavily upon talent from other divisions and the corporate staff during both construction and startup. The importance of the new plant to the whole corporation would justify doing so.

Shutdown and Startup

Inventories were a continuing problem during this phase of the move. Construction and moving schedules changed frequently, as did sales budgets. Each change had to be examined to determine its effect on inventory positions, and potential risk to product franchises.

The transfer of key personnel from the old plants to the new plant created a problem since it was essential to keep the old plants operating at a high level until they were closed. Management had to balance this need against the need to have these key people in Dover during the startup of the new plant. Here again, GF might well have utilized talent from corporate departments or other divisions to manage the final phases of the old plant shutdowns, thus freeing key Jell-O people for the Dover plant.

The magnitude of the Dover start-up job was underestimated. Many unforseeable problems were encountered throughout the entire phase. It required much more time than expected to bring many production lines up to normal operating levels of efficiency. Problems were encountered in shipping and receiving, warehousing, production planning, and other service areas. Much of the equipment—even that moved from the old plants—went through long periods of debugging and modification. The introduction of new products and the need for many "deal" packs of regular products also complicated the start-up phase.

Personnel Policies

The early announcement of plans to consolidate the four plants and the continuing employee information program were highly successful. Employees were informed as soon as the board of directors approved the plan to move. At this stage, the new plant site had not yet been selected. The announcement precluded rumors and misinformation in the plants and was in line with established corporate policy. The initial announcement and several following announcements with regard to the new plant site were made by the General Manager of the Jell-O Division. When the site was selected, a series of "On the Move" bulletins was begun. These were signed by the division operations manager. Fifteen bulletins were issued during the next two years. These contained information on personnel policies, salary and wage rates, construction of the new plant, and so forth.

The decision to offer a job at the new plant—plus generous moving allowances—to everyone was motivated by the need for experienced employees and by management's desire for fair and equitable treatment of all. Additionally, the policy was, in part, responsible for maintaining good employee morale at the four old plants and continuing high production efficiencies which prevailed until the three plants were closed.

An important factor in assisting employees in moving to the new community was the company's provision for a professional adviser on real estate matters. Many employees—particularly long-service, hourly paid personnel—had no previous experience in disposing of or acquiring property. In coming into a new community, they had no adequate yardstick for measuring and comparing property values. Professional assistance eased employee fears and undoubtedly prevented some from making serious blunders.

Just as the company was open and above board with its employees, it was also completely candid with the unions at the Hoboken and Dorchester plants. The primary union, the Amalgamated Food and Allied Workers, also had bargaining units in several other major GF plants, and relations with the union leadership had been good over a long period of time. Union leaders were aware of the fact that the old plants were outmoded, and the company's position on the proposed consolidation was carefully explained to them. As a result, there was no strong opposition to the move, and no disruption of production at the affected plants or any other GF plant. Naturally, the unions moved quickly to organize the new plant. The company consented to an NLRB election at the earliest possible date, and the unions won by a substantial majority. At the time of the new plant dedication, the union's attitude toward the move was illustrated when the company was presented a plaque which stated the union's realization that its success and the jobs of its members depended upon the continuing success of the business.

The company encountered problems in assisting terminated employees in finding other jobs. Some terminated employees were at age levels where they would have considerable difficulty in finding new employment. Many had no experience other than food plant operations, and proposals for retraining programs received little or no employee acceptance. Of course, many female employees were the "second job" holders in their families and were not as strongly motivated to seek new employment as were male employees with families to support.

Some of the problems encountered during the new plant startup might have been minimized if more of the supervisory personnel could have been brought into the picture at an earlier date, such as during preliminary engineering, and allowed to stay with their jobs until the new plant was running smoothly. Some supervisors whose only experience was in small plants undoubtedly had trouble visualizing the complex operation of the consolidated plant before they were put to work and asked to make it run.

Another problem area with supervisory personnel was the fact that men who had been "big frogs in little ponds" at the old plants sometimes ended up several levels from the top of the staff of the new plant. Even though they had more actual responsibility—and probably increased salaries—this was psychological demotion which placed them back on the "working" level.

Public Relations

Closing a plant, particularly one which is important to the economy of a small town, is not easy to accomplish without creating some resentment toward the company. There are ways, however, to cushion the blow and to leave a feeling, when the plant is shut down, that the company has done its best to deal fairly with everyone. A sincere concern for the welfare of employees and the community is essential.

The announcement of a company's intention to close a plant is likely to be greeted with initial shock, disbelief, and even anger. In LeRoy, New York, for example, GF's announcement brought a cry of "We are ruined" from the mayor. And, because Jell-O is a household name, the mayor's reaction made headlines in several newspapers across the country. However, in both LeRoy and Orange, the shock soon abated, to be replaced with an air of calm and feeling that perhaps all was not lost after all. Newspapers began to urge an optimistic "onward and upward" outlook on the part of both communities.

It is important that city officials and civic leaders promptly and fully understand the company's reasons for moving, and there is no better way to accomplish this than a face-to-face meeting between company management and the townspeople's elected representatives. In GF's case, this was done in LeRoy and Orange by the Jell-O Division operations manager who pledged that the company would make every effort to sell the old plants to potential new employers. He also offered to underwrite the cost of a community industrial survey which would help the towns to attract new industry.

GF's attention to the community relations aspects of the consolidation was concentrated largely upon the two small towns where the economic impact was greatest. The local plant manager kept city officials, the press, and radio informed of all important developments as they were announced to employees. Copies of the employee bulletins were given promptly to the press and radio, and there were few prepared news releases. Newspapers often used the bulletins as a basis for staff-written stories quoting liberally from the bulletins and reporting in this way that employees were continuously being informed.

GF's early announcement of plans to build a new plant "within 250 miles of New York City" brought a flood of solicitations and presentations from governors, mayors, chambers of commerce, real estate people, and others. Thousands of letters, telegrams, and telephone calls were received and handled as well as visits from many delegations. Some might question the advisability of announcing the company's plans before a site had been selected for the new plan. However, inasmuch as the rumor mill starts early, GF felt that the benefits of good employee relations and prevention of incorrect assumptions about the proposed move far outweighed the time and effort taken to handle the mountain of inquiries.

Jell-O Division management made the initial contacts with city officials and civic leaders in the new-plant community, and the press was informed that Dover was under serious consideration as the site for the plant although a number of important questions had to be resolved before the decision could be final. Again, some might consider this a premature release of information, arguing that it would be better to defer announcement until a decision had been reached. However, since GF had optioned land, and it was necessary for engineers to work closely with state and city officials in Dover over a period of several months, the news certainly would have leaked out; and there would have been much speculation and rumor in the community instead of facts about what was in progress.

Preparations for announcing the final decision on Dover included letters to employees in the four old plants, a general press release, and a special release keyed to the Dover area. Appropriate GF executives were on hand in Dover to convey the news to state and city officials. Company annual reports, fact books, photographs of company officers, and other supplementary materials were available to interested Dover people. Follow-up events during the next month included a visit to GF headquarters by state and city officials and the press, and a groundbreaking ceremony with the company chairman, the governor, and the mayor doing the honors.

Although GF's public and community relations up until this time were handled by headquarters people, the location of the big new consolidated plant in a relatively small city—this called for someone on the scene who could deal with the community on a day-to-day basis. The company sought and found a person who was both familiar with the community and experienced in public relations.

There was little difficulty in disseminating information about the company and the plant in the new community. People were eager to know; press and radio were cooperative. Numerous civic, service, and social clubs in the new community and the surrounding area invited GF to provide speakers, and this proved to be an excellent means of communicating information about the company.

Dozens of requests for plant tours were received, even before production began. For obvious reasons, these were declined, but always with the promise that an open house would be held as soon as practicable after production began. The date selected for open house, May 1965, was several months after the plant was really in full production and allowed sufficient time to get things in good order for visitors. By that time, the weather was also good.

Planning for a big open house must begin early—as much as a year in advance. Checklists of the endless details that need doing are essential. A "critical path" for such an event is indicated too. Each item on the checklists should be assigned to an individual so that each knows precisely what he is responsible for handling.

In essence, GF's public relations program throughout the move was based on the following: (1) full and early disclosure of all management decisions to employees and the public in that order; (2) involvement of top management through personal contacts with leaders in both the old and new plant communities; (3) continuing communication through bulletins from top management to the affected employees as well as continuing communication at the plant to assist each employee deciding what was in his own best interest; (4) concern for the welfare of the affected communities and earnest attempts to ease the blow; (5) extensive efforts to establish sound relations with new employees and the new community.